CYCLING
Touring Guides

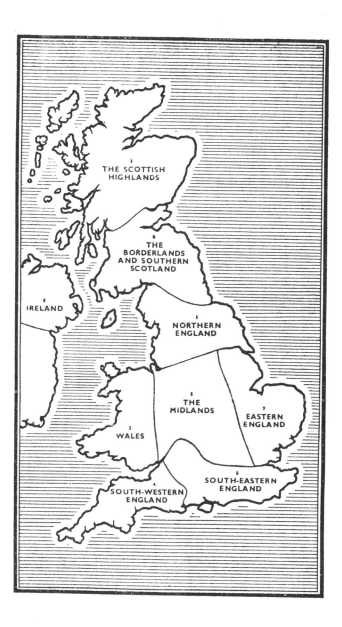

THE SCOTTISH
HIGHLANDS

THE
BORDERLANDS
AND SOUTHERN
SCOTLAND

IRELAND

NORTHERN
ENGLAND

THE
MIDLANDS

EASTERN
ENGLAND

WALES

SOUTH-EASTERN
ENGLAND

SOUTH-WESTERN
ENGLAND

NORTHERN ENGLAND

HAROLD BRIERCLIFFE
WITH MARK JARMAN

BATSFORD

ACKNOWLEDGMENTS

Thanks to Sam Howard at Sustrans for providing details of the latest Sustrans routes, and to Ruth Briercliffe for her assistance.

First Published 1947

Revised edition published 2012 by

Batsford
10 Southcombe Street
London W14 0RA

An imprint of Anova Books Company Ltd

Volume © Batsford, 2012
Additions by Mark Jarman and Sustrans

The moral rights of the author have been asserted.

ISBN-13: 9781849940382

A CIP catalogue record for this book is available from the British Library.

20 19 18 17 16 15 14 13 12
10 9 8 7 6 5 4 3 2

Reproduction by Mission Productions Ltd, Hong Kong
Printed and bound by Toppan Leefung Printing Ltd, China

CONTENTS

LIST OF ILLUSTRATIONS

The scenic illustrations are taken from drawings by Frank Patterson.

LIST OF PLATES

INTRODUCTION

The *Britain by Bike* TV series was based on a collection of old and largely forgotten cycling guides written by Harold Briercliffe over 60 years ago in the late 1940s. Such was the interest in the TV series and associated book that the guides quickly went from almost unknown on the second-hand market to being highly prized and almost impossible to obtain. Perhaps the main reason for the renewed interest in the guides is that they take you back to a time many now see as cycling's golden era. They are much more than dated books with directions to help you find your way from A to B. Indeed anyone who sought out the original *Northern England* guide in the belief that it would provide accurate and reliable information about the best cycle routes in northern England will be rather disappointed. Clearly, as a 21st-century cycling guide, Harold Briercliffe's routes are not as helpful as they were as so many aspects that impact upon cycling have changed dramatically since the 1940s. For this reason, in this revised reissue the end of each chapter includes details of current recommended Sustrans routes that can be used to help explore the places that Briercliffe visited on his cycle journeys. The real joy of Harold's original books is their insight into Britain in an earlier age and they provide a reminder of a gentler pace of life and the attractions of cycle touring around Britain.

The starting point for understanding and appreciating the guides is to look at the context in which they were written. In the post-war years, Harold Briercliffe was a writer for *Cycling* magazine, then the UK's main cycling publication. The guides were assembled from the feature articles written in the magazine, with each issue covering an area of the UK that later formed the basis of a chapter within the regional guides. The first guide was published in 1947 and covered northern England. Over the next few years a further five were produced, ending with the *Southern England* guide, published in 1950.

The post-war Britain that Briercliffe encountered on his cycling journeys was a place in the midst of austerity, where rationing strictly controlled the availability of essentials, including food, clothes and fuel. It is worth remembering that at the end of the 1940s only 1 in 7 households had access to a car. If you were one of the few that did have a car your family's vehicle was likely to have little in common with today's air-conditioned people carriers and 4 x 4s. The most popular cars of the day were rather uncomfortable and modestly sized by modern standards with the Morris Minor and the Austin A30 being two of the most popular 1950s models. For most people, the main methods of mechanised transportation were rail, bus and, of course, the bicycle. With the average workers' holiday being only one or two weeks a year, the bicycle was seen as a key form of transport, offering cheap and easy access to the UK's places of interest (alongside bus and rail). During this period, the UK's cycling industry output was moving towards its peak. Numerous manufacturers produced bicycles not only for the domestic market but for export all over the world. Notable companies from that era include Phillips, Dawes, BSA, Holdsworth, Royal Enfield, Elswick, Sunbeam, Evans, Claud Butler, Bates and Hetchins. But it was Raleigh that became established as the leading bicycle manufacturer of the day with the company's bicycle production reaching a peak of over a million in 1951. This increase in demand and supply was accompanied by advances in design so that bicycles became much more suited to longer distance touring. The use of lightweight 531 tubing to build the classic diamond-shaped frame (including randonneur handlebars), and the introduction of the simplex derailleur gear system and cantilever brakes, meant that the bicycles available in the early 1950s looked remarkably like modern touring bikes (although today's bicycles benefit from sophisticated alloys of steel and aluminium as well as a much greater range of gears).

For those who might have been slightly less enthusiastic about spending their leisure time on a bike, there was relatively little to encourage them to stay indoors. This was a world without games consoles, personal stereos, home computers or wide-screen TVs. By the beginning of the 1950s only 8% of households in the UK had a TV. For the few television owners, there was only one station (ITV did not join the BBC until 1955) and the broadcasting hours were very limited. So for the vast majority, the radio 'wireless' provided the main source of family entertainment within the home. Cinema was the only other boom area for entertainment.

Against this background of ongoing rationing and limited forms of entertainment, it is perhaps easier to understand the reasons why Harold Briercliffe (approaching 40) embarked on the monumental task of covering the whole of the UK by bike. Following production of the Northern England guide in 1947, Briercliffe's articles in *Cycling* magazine were gradually used to form a series of regional guides covering the Scottish Highlands, Wales, south west England, and the Midlands before finishing with southern England.

Briercliffe defined the area covered by his *Northern England* guide as primarily covering the Lake District, the Yorkshire Dales and the North East Coast with shorter tours over the Pennines and across to the Lancashire Coast. It is a region of some variety although relatively compact and does not include some areas to the north of the Midlands (including parts of Lancashire and Cheshire), which Briercliffe decided should be featured within the vast area included in his *Midlands* guide. The introduction to the *Northern England* guide was written by Harry England, then the well-established editor of *Cycling*, Britain's weekly cycling newspaper, which was first published in 1891. The introduction is very much of its time, painting post-war Britain at the dawn of a new era. Harry England looks optimistically towards the future, stating that the new series of Briercliffe's touring guides had been designed for a modern type of cyclist looking to travel longer distances and basing these tours on the increasing availability of bed-and-breakfast accommodation and youth hostels in the countryside.

In 1940s Britain it was certainly difficult to anticipate the extent and pace of the changes over the next 60 years, particularly in terms of housing and traffic growth. Briercliffe suggests the use of what are now very busy 'A' roads to cycle out of main urban areas. In the *Northern England* guide he does not mention the unsuitability of A roads because of high-volume traffic. Similarly he makes no reference to the need to avoid the M1 and M62 motorway network around Leeds, or the M6 to the northwest, because in 1950 Britain's motorway network was still very much on the drawing board. In 1946 the first map was published showing the planned motorway system, including the M1, M4, M5, M6, M62 and M18. In the same year, the government announced an 80% expansion of the trunk road system, adding 3,500 miles to the network. A series of trunk-road improvements took place throughout the 1950s, a decade which ended with the opening of the M1 in November 1959.

This gradual increase in Britain's highway capacity coincided with the growth in car ownership and use. The Department for Transport has recorded levels of use of the various types of transport (in annual billion vehicle kms) every year since 1949. Cycling has declined rapidly since the 1950s from a high of 24 billion vehicle kms in 1949 to around 5 billion vehicle kms in 2010. In the same 61-year period, car usage has risen from just over 20 billion vehicle kms in 1949 to almost 400 billion vehicle kms by 2010. Against this backdrop, it is little wonder that the road conditions Briercliffe describes at the end of the 1940s bear so little relationship to what would be found if you tried cycle touring on Britain's trunk roads today.

In addition, Britain experienced significant house building in the postwar years, leading to the expansion of major urban conurbations as well as some of our smaller towns and cities. There are many reminders of the obvious changes that have occurred since the 1940s in Briercliffe's description of the places he visits on his journeys. Briercliffe's route from London towards the Midlands and the North passed through Stevenage, which had recently been designated a New Town by the New Towns Act of 1946. Stevenage was transformed from a town of around 6000 people to a major urban area with a population of over 80,000. The 1946 Act resulted in similar levels of development in a ring of New Towns around London, with places such as Bracknell, Crawley, Hemel Hempstead, Basildon and Harlow all growing rapidly. Further north, the first generation of New Towns included Newton Aycliffe and Peterlee. A second wave of new-town building followed in the 1960s with the most significant northern England development at Washington, Tyne and Wear. The focus remained on development further south, however, with the largest at Milton Keynes.

You might wonder whether, in the face of so much housing development, road building and traffic growth since 1950, if any of the UK that Briercliffe discovered on his journeys still exists. It is therefore reassuring to find that so much of the distinctive character of Briercliffe's Britain can still be discovered by the cycle tourist. This applies more to Northern England than many other parts of the UK (most notably the South East) which have been subject to far greater development pressures. Much of the landscape identified by Briercliffe in his Northern England guide has also been protected by its designation as National Park land. The Lake District, Yorkshire Dales, North York Moors and Northumberland are amongst four of the ten National parks that were designated by Government in 1949. In the period since the time of the legislation, strict planning controls have limited the amount of development so that much of the varied landscape described by Briercliffe remains as it was in the 1940s. The last sixty years represents a mere blink of an eye in comparison to the millions of years over which the geological foundation of the Lake District or Yorkshire Dales was formed. The mix of rock types, including limestone, sandstone and granite, have a significant impact on the ecology of the area and these contrasts can still be viewed when cycling from the Lake District through to the Dales. The touring cyclist will discover that the physical characteristics remain unchanged in the sense that the heights of the main Lakeland mountains are as they were stated by Briercliffe, together with the altitude of the passes and the dimensions of the lakes.

What has changed, of course, is the level of traffic on the network of roads crossing the Lake District and the Yorkshire Dales. Many of the on-road routes mentioned by Briercliffe (particularly in the Lake District) are no longer suitable for leisure cycling. In contrast, the network of off-road cycle routes is now much more extensive than it was 60 years ago. Back in the 1940s Briercliffe was keen to emphasise that the off-road tracks and paths were steep and rocky and generally uncomfortable for cycling. This explains why one chapter of Briercliffe's guide was devoted to 'Pass-Storming' – an approach to off-road cycling involving picking up and carrying your bike along the roughest and steepest sections of path. It is interesting to read Briercliffe's advice about how to tackle pass-storming in an era well before mountain bikes. Another chapter is called "Hill Climbing on Foot", advising the Lake District cyclist "to discard his bicycle whenever he can and climb a hill." Given that traffic levels in the Lake District are considerably higher than they were 60 years ago and that the off-road alternatives for cyclists are now much more extensive it makes sense for today's cyclists to refer to the Sustrans route information included at the end of each chapter if embarking on Lake District cycling.

Briercliffe's account of cycling in the Yorkshire Dales provides an interesting contrast to the Lake District. It has a more contemporary feel in the sense that much of the surrounds can still be enjoyed using the minor-road network identified in the guide. The minor road network continues to provide some suitable links to many of the villages that Briercliffe describes with such affection. Particular favourites of Briercliffe's were Clapham, Burnsall, Wensley, Arncliffe and Masham with Keld being singled out as the best of the bunch. One aspect of cycling in the Dales that has diminished is the easy availability of cheap overnight accommodation. Bed-and-breakfast places are, of course, still widely available (although not at an average price of six shillings a night!) but the number of rural youth hostels has dramatically reduced as a result of the Youth Hostel Association's (YHA) closure programme. This would not have been anticipated by Briercliffe back in the late 1940s when membership of the Youth Hostel Association (YHA) was heading towards its peak. At the start of the 1950s there were 303 youth hostels and over 200,000 YHA members. Increased availability of holidays abroad and changes in the level of walking and hiking resulted in a gradual fall in demand for YHA accommodation. This led to closures and a modernisation programme with the emphasis on providing better youth-hostel facilities in towns and cities. Around 100 of the hostels (particularly those in more remote rural areas) were closed. Today's touring cyclists planning a holiday in the Lake District or elsewhere in northern England should check with the YHA to see which of Briercliffe's recommended youth hostels are still available.

Travelling beyond the Yorkshire Dales through the North York Moors and on to the North East coast, Briercliffe suggests a number of routes that have since become much less suitable for cycling. Today the route options include an ideal traffic-free path, which was the Scarborough and Whitby Railway line, which first opened in 1885. The railway line was closed in 1965 as a casualty of the infamous 'Beeching Axe' which fell in the 1960s and resulted in the closure of more than 4,000 miles of railway branch lines and 3,000 stations. In the last few decades some of these old railway routes have been converted to form excellent paths for cyclists and pedestrians. As cycle routes, they have become a much-valued facility, free from the hazards of fast-moving motor vehicles and are generally very flat, not exceeding a gradient of more than about 1 in 20. So today's reader wanting to revisit the 'Centres in Yorkshire' described by Briercliffe would be well advised to consider using routes such as the popular Scarborough to Whitby cycle path, which forms part of the Sustrans National Cycle Route 1 (see page 108).

In Harold's final chapters there are plenty of reminders of the variety of landscape and surroundings in Northern England. Briercliffe recommends exploring the Lancashire coastline from Liverpool northwards. He sets out a day tour taking in an area that includes Southport, described as 'a large and rather select seaside resort', as well as Blackpool and the area inland from Morecambe Bay. This area has experienced significant traffic growth over the last 60 years with the development of an extensive motorway network, including the M6, M55 and M65 as well as the expansion of the general trunk-road system. While some of Briercliffe's suggested routes are therefore no longer appropriate, there is a network of recently designated cycle routes, such as National Cycle Route 62 (see page 150) and Regional Routes 90/91 (see page 136), which provide an excellent option for exploring the area. Travelling across the Yorkshire Dales, Briercliffe seems very keen on encouraging cyclists to visit the city of York. His description of The Shambles and other streets around York Minster still seems reasonably accurate 60 years later. The York Minster restoration scheme means the impressive cathedral remains much as Briercliffe described even though the building was engulfed in fire in 1984. The importance of the city's chocolate manufacturing has certainly declined from the 1950s when the output from two companies, Rowntree and Terry's, was so great that York was known as Chocolate City. No doubt Briercliffe would be pleased to know that York was recently designated 'Cycling City' with almost £4 million provided by the government to increase cycling facilities and encourage access by bike to many of the city's wonderful historic places and buildings.

Mark Jarman
2012

FOREWORD
By
H. H. England
Editor of *Cycling*

IN the past twenty years the development of the Youth Hostels Association has brought into the field of cycle touring an entirely new type of cyclist, and the popularity of the sport is growing with the passing of every year.

Many guide books published hitherto, while being excellent and informative within their own sphere, have ignored the fact that for the cyclist a very special approach is needed. It is to meet these particular requirements that this present series of touring guides, written by a cyclist with some twenty-five years of touring experience behind him, has been designed.

For this reason the author has not aimed at being comprehensive, but has preferred to discriminate in his choice of routes and centres so that the newcomer to the sport may be given a clear and simple lead in his task of discovering the countryside. And while, for example, only one of the several routes up Helvellyn is described, considerable space is devoted to the technique of "pass-storming"— a feature of particular interest to the cyclist and conspicuously absent from previous works.

This guide to Northern England is to be followed by companion volumes, until the whole of the British Isles has been brought within their scope, and it is to be hoped that they will prove as useful in informing the cyclist about our British countryside as the *Cycling Manual* and *Cycling Book of Maintenance* have been in introducing him to his own machine.

PART I

THE LAKE DISTRICT

INTRODUCTION

THE scenery of England reaches its highest level in the Lake District, the north-west corner of the country that comprises parts of Cumberland, Westmorland and the Furness District of Lancashire. Within a ring that is no more than 20 miles across at its broadest is to be found nearly every type of country, from the nobility of the highest mountains in England, by the contrasted charm of lakes and tarns, through a whole series of landscapes that attract the eye, in hillside, stream, fall, seashore and moorland. Kendal, Penrith, Cockermouth and Broughton-in-Furness are nearly, but not quite, the corners of a rectangle that encloses all the scenic beauty of Lakeland.

Yet within this small area is to be found such riches, so little dullness, that it does not suffer in comparison with other and more noted touring regions. In Lakeland everything—or nearly everything—seems to be in accord. Proportion rather than height or width gives the Lakeland mountains their unique charm, coupled with the fact that most of the giants amongst the hills can be seen from foot to head at a glance. Into these massive frames fit the lakes themselves, with their many tributary streams and waterfalls. Amidst these hills water is always sparkling and fresh, as the builders of reservoirs know only too well. Both Thirlmere and Haweswater now slake Manchester's thirst.

Lakeland is not cyclists' country in the same way as the Yorkshire Dales or North Wales. The central valleys mostly run up into the knot of hills which rises to **Scafell Pike**. Through main routes are few, with the exception of the main Kendal-Windermere-Ambleside-Keswick highway, which serves as an artery that during the summer is too congested with motor traffic to be popular with the cyclist.

The rider who thinks that he can tour Lakeland as he would Devon and Cornwall, or even the West Highlands, by riding from one main road junction to another at high speed will find that he has gone through the region in half a day, and will probably end by wondering why there is such a 'to-do' about the English Lake District.

No district in Britain is better seen by the cyclist from a centre, or several centres, than Lakeland. Indeed, while the writer does not agree with those people who say that the Lakes cannot be seen otherwise than by walking, he believes that the tourist who deserts his bicycle to climb hills or to explore valleys or to row will get nearer to the heart of the Lake country than those who cling faithfully to two wheels. If it can be arranged, a Lakeland week might consist of two nights in the Elterwater area west of Grasmere (for the south side of the District), three nights about **Derwentwater** or in **Borrowdale** (for the north), and two nights around Strands, at the foot of Wastwater or in Eskdale (for the south-west). From and between these points he will be able to see all the large lakes with the exception of Haweswater, which is still suffering from the building of Manchester's second Lakeland reservoir—and which can be left out of a week's tour.

Accommodation of all kinds is plentiful, ranging from palatial hydros to homely farmhouses. There are over 20 youth hostels too, most of them situated in parts of the district that are of especial beauty. The family man will find in the small resorts of **Ravenglass**, Seascale and St. Bees seaside quarters that are within short distances of some of the best of Lakeland scenery. A word of warning is necessary, however, about accommodation at holiday times, such as Easter, Christmas and the months of July and August. Those who wish to visit Lakeland at these times would be advised to book well in advance. This warning applies particularly to the youth hostels in the central area, at places like Grasmere and Borrowdale.

The main roads of the Lake District are now as smooth as those of other districts of Britain. Even the roads up the side valleys that are virtual culs-de-sac are now, for the most part, tarred. These minor highways are nearly always narrow and winding, as well as undulating, but as these conditions cause the majority of motorists to be cautious, there is little danger on them. Cyclists should take heed, however, of the danger-boards at the head of hills—they mean all that they say in the Lake District.

Notable as exceptions to the rule that the minor roads are now smooth are the two road passes of Wrynose and Hardknott, on the only direct east-to-west route between Ambleside and the west coast north of Barrow. These roads were barred to tourists during part of the war, and their surfaces remain rutted and riddled with watercourses. The true cycle-tourist does not object to the element of adventure and the comparative solitude that results from this state of affairs.

Other road passes that remain rough are the Garburn, east of Windermere, and the Eskdale to Ulpha road. The Kirkstone Pass is no longer formidable on account of its surface, and the same applies to that part of the trunk highway between Kendal and Keswick which crosses Dunmail Raise. Whinlatter Pass, from Keswick westwards, is also smooth, while the Newlands Hause route, between Buttermere and Newlands, is good, too. The most dangerous road pass for cyclists in the entire Lake District is without doubt Honister. Both sides of this pass are steep, and since they were modernized with neat road edges and tarred surfaces, they have encouraged high speeds on the descents that have led to fatal accidents to cyclists. The west (or Buttermere) slope is particularly deceptive, for there an initial length of steep fall leads to a more gradual drop that has vicious leftwards and rightwards twists across a bridge which cannot be taken at high speeds.

Of the Lakes themselves, it should be said that while Windermere is the longest and most accessible of them all (10½ miles in length), Derwentwater the most beautiful of the larger ones, and **Wastwater** the wildest, some of the smaller sheets, notably Loweswater and **Tarn Hows** (near Coniston) form miniatures that are often lovelier than their larger rivals.

Nearly all the summits in Lakeland are worth climbing afoot for the experience or the views, but the two which the writer finds most satisfying are domelike Great Gable (2,949 ft. above sea level), between Borrowdale and Wastwater, in the very core of Lakeland, and Helvellyn (3,118 ft.), between Ullswater and Thirlmere, although for variety and richness the panorama from Coniston Old Man (2,635 ft,) is hard to beat. The highest hill in England is Scafell Pike (3,210 ft.), which with its neighbour Scafell (3,162 ft.) forms one of the finest of all regions in Britain for rough scrambling afoot.

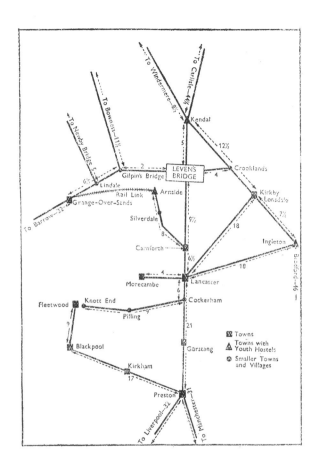

**Approaches to Leven's Bridge for the Lake District
(Diagram not to scale)**

In a district of such abundant rain and steep and rocky slopes, waterfalls abound. Some of them, such as **Lodore Falls**, between Keswick and Borrowdale, on the east side of Derwentwater, are disappointing, except after a heavy downpour. Others, like **Scale Force**—a longish walk from Buttermere village—are not very easy of access for the cyclist. A number of the falls, such as Colwith Force, between Ambleside and Little Langdale, and Tilberthwaite Gill, north of Coniston, is quite approachable and worth exploration. Perhaps the finest waterfall of all in the Lake District is **Dalegarth Force** (Stanley Gill), rather obscurely situated south of Boot, in Eskdale.

APPROACHES

Windermere Station, some eight miles beyond Kendal, situated on a branch of the L.M.S. main line from Euston, at Oxenholme, is the handiest of railheads on the south side of the district. Tourists who prefer a more unorthodox and quieter approach could do far worse than travel to Cark or Ulverston on the former Furness Railway, and reach the mountains and lakes by one of the easy south-north valleys.

Another railway route, this time to the best centre in the northern part of the Lake District, would be by the Euston-Glasgow main line to Penrith, there changing for Keswick, and thus avoiding the hard and somewhat dreary ride along the Penrith-Keswick highway. This approach would also serve for riders approaching by train from Glasgow and Edinburgh. Rather more out of the way, but introducing the tourist to the relatively unknown scenery of the Eden Valley, is the approach that uses Appleby as its railhead. Riders from the Midland towns of Nottingham, Derby and Sheffield would find this handy, and so would those of the Leeds and Bradford area, as a number of fast trains on the old Midland route into Scotland via Skipton, Hellifield, Hawes Junction and Appleby stop at the latter town, itself the sleepiest and quaintest of county capitals.

Of road approaches, the handiest of all from London is by way of Dunstable, Towcester, the Daventry and Coventry by-passes, Stonebridge (turn right), Coleshill, Lichfield, Rugeley, Newcastle-under-Lyme, Talke (turn left), Knutsford, Warrington, Wigan, Preston, Lancaster, Carnforth, Leven's Bridge and Kendal. This, however, is the main road taken by the motor lorries between London and the Midlands, Lancashire and Scotland, and is inclined to be crowded at times. Nevertheless, it passes through few large towns, and is fast and smooth throughout. A recommended short cut to Bowness-on-Windermere, avoiding Kendal, is to turn left at Leven's Bridge, five miles south of Kendal, and to go via Gilpin's Bridge (turn right) and the Lyth Valley and Winster. Using either of these approaches, the distance from London to Windermere is only a little shorter than 250 miles. Manchester (by Walkden and Chorley) is 82 miles away, and so also is Liverpool (by Ormskirk and Rufford).

From Leeds and Bradford, the main but interesting road approach to Windermere is via Skipton, Settle and Kirkby Lonsdale, less than 80 miles from both centres.

From Carlisle (and Glasgow and Edinburgh) to Keswick there is a hilly approach route by Bothel, 31 miles, while from Newcastle to Keswick the road is by Hexham, Alston and Penrith (82 miles).

The Lakes

Lake	Greatest length	Greatest breadth	Height above sea level
	miles	miles	ft.
Windermere	10½	1	130
Ullswater	7½	¾	476
Coniston	5¼	½	143
Bassenthwaite	4½	¾	223
Derwentwater	3	1⅛	244
Wastwater	3	½	200
Crummock Water	2½	⅝	321
Ennerdale Water	2½	¾	368
Thirlmere	3¼	½	533
Esthwaite Water	1½	⅜	217
Buttermere	1¼	⅜	329
Loweswater	1¼	⅜	429
Grasmere	1	½	208
Rydal Water	¾	¼	181
Brothers Water	⅜	¼	520

A FOUR-DAY TOUR IN THE
LAKE DISTRICT
(From Leven's Bridge, or Windermere, and back—156½ miles)

THE basis of a Lakeland tour of up to a month's duration is a girdle that starts and finishes at Leven's Bridge or Windermere. This round can be accomplished in four days at the expense of not seeing Ullswater, Haweswater or Bassenthwaite, but nevertheless gives nearly a complete picture of the Lake District to the cyclist in a hurry. Leven's Bridge is chosen as a jumping-off place because from it the road westwards leads almost at once into unfrequented lanes, whereas the main route through Kendal is busy throughout the holiday period. Those starting from Windermere Station can link up with the suggested basic route at Hawkshead (reached via the regular vehicular ferry from Bowness to Far Sawrey) and return to Windermere Station via Newby Bridge and Bowness at the end of the tour.

Cyclists travelling from the West Riding via Settle can turn leftwards off the Kirkby Lonsdale road at Crooklands and follow a short but somewhat involved lane route to Leven's Bridge. Scottish and Newcastle riders can join the tour at Keswick and follow it round in an anti-clockwise direction.

Leven's Bridge is on the A6 route from London to Carlisle, 37 miles north of Preston. Leven's Hall is on the right approaching the bridge. It has interesting historical associations, and is open to visitors occasionally. Turn left just beyond the bridge from which the road leads across the mosses (the local name for marshes) to **Gilpin's Bridge** (2 miles from Leven's Bridge); left again, with the road still level, to Lindale (6½), where right, climbing at first, by Higher Newton to Newby Bridge (11½), delightfully situated at the foot of Lake Windermere.

Cross the bridge to the west and least-frequented side of the lake, where the road passes through dense woodland with occasional glimpses of the water. At the first fork turn right and also at second, but at third, turn left, away from lake, in the direction of Hawkshead.

Emerging on the west side of Esthwaite Water, reach the village of Hawkshead (21), one of the quaintest in Lancashire, 'all angles, twists and crooks'. The small church on a little hill south of the village occupies the site of a Norman edifice, and probably dates from Elizabethan times.

Less than half a mile northwards, turn left up the Coniston road, and after a mile, near the top of the rise, turn right at the signpost for Tarn Hows, an attractive small lake mirroring the woods and hills. Keep left around the south side and then descend a rough road (caution) that re-emerges on the Hawkshead-Coniston highway. Then go round the head of Lake Coniston to Coniston (26).

The district is partly spoilt by slate quarrying, but **Coniston Water**, the third longest lake (5¼ miles), and **Coniston Old Man** (2,633 ft.) are worth exploration.

Leave by the Ambleside road, following romantic Yewdale Beck, which runs below steep crags and through thick woodland. At High Yewdale bend left up the valley, leaving the main road. The scenery hereabouts is rugged, quite like a Highland glen, with rocky gills and many trees. At the foot of **Tilberthwaite Gill** (28½ miles—2½ from Coniston) leave your bicycles and climb the gorge to the left (don't be deterred by quarry debris) by means of ladders, bridges, ramps and stairs. The ravine is about 200 yds. long and its sides are rough and sheer. At the last bridge there is a long and picturesque fall.

Continuing awheel, the rough lane leads by High Tilberthwaite, still in romantic surroundings, and then into **Little Langdale** (31 miles).

NOTE. The tourist who wishes to avoid the larger towns should note that no definite halting-place is recommended for the night, Little Langdale being used for the sake of marking a definite point. The whole area around Little Langdale, Great Langdale, Elterwater and down to Ambleside is recommended for this purpose. There are youth hostels at Grasmere, Ambleside, Coniston and south of Hawkshead.

Continue westwards ('the Wrynose' road) from Little Langdale village to a fork just short of Fell Foot Farm. Here take the right-hand road and up a steep rise to **Blea Tarn**. The peaks ahead are the famous

Langdale Pikes. Although denuded of many trees by war-time felling, the Tarn, with the background of the Pikes, forms a splendid picture. Extreme caution is needed on the sharp descent into Langdale at Wall End. Join the Great Langdale road at Middle Fell Place, where turn rightwards. Westwards is the wild, mountainous trough of Mickleden, leading to Rossett Ghyll, fiercest of all Lakeland pass-storming routes, and the Stake Pass, the latter rather easier (see page 35).

Blea Tarn and the Langdale Pikes

The run down the Great Langdale Valley is delightful. Less than a mile on look out for **Dungeon Ghyll** on the left. Leave your bicycles and explore the ghyll, where a thread of water falls between perpendicular rocks that are a hundred feet high.

Regaining the bicycles, it is worthwhile *en route* to Chapel Stile village (38 miles from Leven's Bridge) looking back at the **Pike o' Stickle**, the most westerly of the Pikes, which rises some 1,800 ft. from foot to summit. Slate quarries mar the valley hereabouts. At **Chapel Stile** fork left, off the main valley road, and along a fine ledge across an open common, and so around hairpins on a stiff climb to the summit (420 ft.), where a grand view of the whole arc of hills round from the Lancashire Fells, by Bowfell to the Langdale Pikes, spreads to the south.

About 150 yds. down the subsequent descent, **Loughrigg Terrace**, giving lovely views across the Vale of Grasmere, is well worth a halt and a walk.

The drop to the side of Grasmere Lake is down the short but very steep Red Bank and into Grasmere (41 miles).

Go northwards (right at the massive but simple church—quite in keeping with the setting) to the main Ambleside-Keswick road at the Swan Inn. Then left, up the long drag of Dunmail Raise (782 ft.), a rise of two miles from the Swan. This is the most important road gap in Lakeland, crossing the boundary between Westmorland and Cumberland. A pile of stones (to the left of the road summit) is said to cover the remains of Dunmail, last King of Cumberland.

An easy descent leads to Thirlmere, where the main road should be forsaken by going left along the 'new' road, 5¼ miles long, keeping to the west side of the reservoir, which serves Manchester with water by means of an aqueduct 95¾ miles long, opened in 1894. The road here runs beneath crags, but the plantations of conifers often come between the road and lake, although there are frequent breaks at points of particular interest. The dam is 260 yds. in length and 100 ft. high from foundation to parapet. The new highway meets the main road 4¼ miles from Keswick. The recommended west-side route is almost a mile longer than the main road. A stretch of undulating road finishes with the sudden descent on **Keswick** (55 miles).

NOTE While Keswick is mentioned as the stopping place for the night, the whole of the surrounding country district provides accommodation as well. Borrowdale and its side valleys, Grange, Swinside, Braithwaite, Applethwaite and the Vale of St. John, all within 40 minutes by bicycle from Keswick, are recommended. There are youth hostels at Keswick, in Borrowdale (two), and at the top of the Honister Pass.

Travel southwards from Keswick along the east side of Derwentwater. Some two miles down the road, on the left, are **Barrow Falls**, situated in private grounds (permission to view generally granted), and then after another mile are the Falls of Lodore (a small charge is made for viewing), only worth seeing, like Barrow

Falls, after a heavy downpour. During the run alongside Derwentwater there are splendid impressions of the National Trust property at Brandelhow Park, on the opposite shore, and the shapely form of the hill called Catbells. Behind this range is the curious peak of Causey Pike. (Grange-in-Borrowdale, just right of the main route; has a two-eyed bridge which leads into the village and on to Brandelhow Park.)

Five miles from Keswick, a rough but rideable track turns left to the **Bowder Stone**, a boulder weighing some 2,000 tons that is poised on a delicate edge. A ladder may be used to reach the top of the stone. The main route is rejoined by continuing along the track. Borrowdale is here a combination of crag and wood and stream, and most romantic. **Rosthwaite** (6½ miles—6½ from Keswick) is well situated, and then comes **Seatoller**, at the foot of the Honister Pass. The road has been remade and resurfaced in recent years, and after the first steep ascent through woods, the gradient eases on the open moorland. There is a youth hostel at the head of the pass (1,176 ft.). The striking face of Honister Crag to the left is partly spoilt by the presence of slate quarries.

Heights of Falls

Fall	Location	Feet
Scale Force	Buttermere	123
Barrow	Grange-in-Borrowdale	108
Stock Ghyll Force	Ambleside	100
Lodore	Grange-in-Borrowdale	90
Aira Force	Ullswater	70
Dalegarth Force	Eskdale	60
Dungeon Ghyll	Great Langdale	60
Colwith Force	Little Langdale	45

The greatest caution is needed on the descent of Honister Pass because of an awkward bridge about 1¾ miles down. The smooth road surface encourages dangerously high speeds.

The highway flattens out by the north side of Buttermere, a more austere lake than any seen previously. **Buttermere** village (69 miles) is the starting point of the walk to Scale Force, about two miles west (see page 19).

After a short strath (the floor of a wide valley), **Crummock Water** is approached. Seen from the headland at Buttermere Hause Point (a mile north-west of Buttermere village), Crummock Water is one of the most imposing and picturesque of the lakes. The whole range on the far (or south-west) side of the lake is graceful and impressive.

The road climbs away from Crummock Water by Lanthwaite Green and Brackenthwaite, half a mile beyond which the way turns sharply round to the left and down to **Scale Hill Hotel**. Between typical north-country stone walls, the route ascends and then drops on **Loweswater** one of the smallest and also one of the most picturesque of the lakes.

Thereafter the country is mediocre and the lanes at times confusing, especially round by Lamplugh Church and Crossdale to **Ennerdale Bridge** (83), on the fringe of the West Cumberland industrial district. Two miles from Ennerdale Bridge is the **Angler's Inn**, at the foot of Ennerdale Water, overlooking one of the wildest and grandest of the Lakeland scenes. This area is threatened by a scheme for a waterworks. Return to Ennerdale Bridge (87).

From Ennerdale Bridge climb across Cold Fell, along a lonely road (not recommended for after-dark travel) to Calder Abbey, the scanty ruins of which are worth a visit.

On to Calder Bridge (91) and by Gosforth, where there is a 7th-century cross in the churchyard, to Strands or Nether Wasdale (100).

NOTE. The finest resort, scenically, in West Cumberland, is Wasdale Head, but the accommodation there is frequently fully booked during the height of the summer and at holiday times. Alternatives to the farmhouse quarters at Strands or Nether Wasdale are to be found on the coast, at Seascale or Ravenglass, or in Eskdale.

Proceed along the shore of Wastwater, passing first (from Strands) through the luxuriant woods of Wasdale Hall. On emerging by the lake shore, the scene is wild to the extreme. Across the lake the coloured Screes, topped by dark crags, form the principal feature of the view. As one goes along the lakeside, however, the razor edge of the jutting hill called Yewbarrow, on the near side of Wastwater, becomes pronounced. Beyond the head of the lake there is a strath, with green fields and many criss-crossing walls, between impressive fells. Scafell Pike and its spur of Lingmell are on the right, the cone of Great Gable straight ahead, and Kirkfell and Yewbarrow to the left. **Wasdale Head** (106—6 from Strands) is a base for climbers, with a tiny church and an inn.

Return to Strands (112) and then go to Santon Bridge and **Eskdale Green**. The miniature railway is again taking passengers from Boot to Ravenglass occasionally during the summer months after war-time closing. The engine sheds at Ravenglass are open for inspection.

Continue up Eskdale, a delightful valley, by **Boot**, which is the starting-point for the walk to Dalegarth Force. Beyond the Woolpack Inn up the steep and rough ascent of Hardknott Pass (about 1¼ miles of stiff climbing), note on a spur, to the left after opening the first gate, a Roman camp, including slight traces of a bath, temple and parade ground. Rather higher up the pass it is worth leaving the bicycle to inspect them.

Beware of corners on the far drop of a mile. There is a fine view down the Duddon valley, or Dunnerdale (to right), and towards the mountain fastnesses to the left of the road leading across the Wrynose Pass (ahead). Cross the bridge to the farm of **Cockley Beck** (124). Go rightwards down Dunnerdale along a gated road that is now smooth-surfaced, by Dale Head (youth hostel) and through Seathwaite to **Ulpha** (131), on an exciting little highway that keeps close to the Duddon and drops most of the way. Then, on wider roads, to **Broughton-in-Furness** (135).

Make in an easterly direction by Grizebeck, Lowick Green and Haverthwaite to **Newby Bridge** (145 miles), and then along the outward route by **Higher Newton, Lindale** and **Gilpin's Bridge** to Leven's Bridge (156½).

The four-day tour given here is strenuous—only practicable for the fit. Those wishing to take their time on the round could arrange additional night breaks in the journey at **Buttermere, Ennerdale**

Newby Bridge

or around Broughton-in-Furness, thus making a week's journey and assuring themselves of a comprehensive impression of the district. Those with more time at their disposal are directed to the day tours, starting on page 35.

LAKELAND PASS-STORMING FOR THE CYCLIST

Pass-storming by bicycle is such an individual matter that the writer proposes to deal with the topic in the first person singular. The pastime has been criticized as dangerous and as hard work, mostly by those who have never attempted it. That there is danger I will not deny, but it is no worse than anything the walker who goes exploring the fells may encounter: such hazards as there are arise from the weather, particularly from mist, snow or frost, and just as no experienced walker would commence a crossing in such conditions, neither would any sensible pass-stormer. Moreover, it cannot be over-emphasized that no cyclist who is not both wise and experienced in both cycling and walking should go rambling about on the Lakeland hills alone, with or without a bicycle, in any sort of weather conditions.

As for the fetish of hard work, there is no sport that is not hard work at times. Football, cricket, tennis, walking, road and track racing, rock climbing, all demand an output of energy which is never considered objectionable.

There are three considerations that make pass-storming worthwhile. The first is that by using footpaths instead of roads, the true lover of the country gets right away from the noise of the main roads and into the heart of the mountain country. His lightweight bicycle is not a great hindrance, certainly not much more so than the immense rucksacks that some of the walking fraternity adopt. The second is that in many parts of the country (but not, unfortunately, on some of the Lakeland passes) there are many miles of narrow footpaths that provide exciting and engrossing cycling. (The track eastwards down Glen Affric, in the north-west Highlands, from the Camban bothy, is one example, and another is the footpath through the Wessenden Valley, between Marsden, in the West Riding, and the Isle of Skye Inn.) Finally, in the Lake District especially, the cyclist who keeps exclusively to roads is bound sooner or later to reach a valley-head and wish that he need not return by the way he came. It is a convenience to be able to carry or push a bicycle six miles instead of retracing 40 or 50 miles of a roundabout route.

Before I describe the pass-storming routes, I had best mention some things that are fairly obvious but, nevertheless, inclined to be overlooked. First of all, a lightweight bicycle and a lightweight kit are advisable. I have been over the Sty Head Pass with a tandem, full camping kit and a very muscular girl partner. I have seen others in the Larig Ghru Pass similarly placed. I would say now, however, keep the weight down as much as possible and use singles.

Although on a fine midsummer day the Lakeland fells are busy enough with walkers, on bad days and in winter these are few and far between. Hence, as a general rule, I would recommend that no pass-stormer should travel alone. Company is encouraging and a partner may, on some occasion, be worth a great deal.

The same advice as is given in the next chapter for the walking explorer (the need for map, watch, compass, food, etc.) applies just as much to the cycling pass-stormer.

I have never yet removed my pedals before the worst of pass-storming routes, and have not required to take ropes and straps as some of my more enterprising and provident friends have done. Where the bicycle has to be carried (as *down* Rossett Ghyll), it should be slung with the top tube across the right shoulder. I have known pass-stormers who carried their bicycles over both shoulders pick-a-back. But these were supermen! It is best to remove pump and lamps and place them safely in the saddlebag.

I have listed all the highest Lakeland Passes on the following page. Curiously enough, I have crossed them all, with the exception of the highest, the Sticks Pass. I might modestly add, therefore, at this juncture, that I have never gone in for pass-storming as a vainglorious pursuit, since I have never even thought of crossing the Sticks, as it has never been convenient to do so. All the information about the foot passes given here is based, therefore, on personal experience, except for the details of the Sticks, which are based on the report of a friend who has made quite a hobby of the crossing of this pass.

Both distances and times are given for the journeys from start to finish. The latter are a more useful measure and are to be regarded as an average time. Some of the more energetic will beat certain of the average times quite handsomely. Others will find them much too optimistic.

All the road passes, except for the Wrynose and Garburn, are described elsewhere. The Wrynose Pass is a hard road climb between Little Langdale and Cockley Beck, while the Garburn Pass connects the rather remote valley of Kentmere (on the way to the Nan Bield Pass from the south) with Windermere.

THE FOOT PASSES

The **Sticks Pass** links the Ullswater district with Thirlspot. Its main value is that it provides a route between Ullswater and the district south of Keswick without using the busy main roads by Threlkeld on the one hand and Kirkstone and Dunmail Raise on the other.

Turn off the Patterdale-Pooley Bridge highway, about a mile south of the former place, up Glenridding. About half a mile onwards turn right and shortly left and climb for a mile to the Greenside Lead Mill. Bend rightwards a little ahead (turning off the Keppel Cove route to Helvellyn). Climb around the north side of the reservoir and then strike westwards above the beck to the summit. A number of upright sticks at the head of the pass gave it its name.

On the descent, gradually bear rightwards. Hereabouts the track is vague, but about 1,000 ft. below the summit it is again easily distinguishable. There is no riding on the descent, but the track throughout does not demand much carrying of the bicycle. The final drop alongside the Stanah Beck (on the right) is steep, and a road is joined close to where the lane down St. John's in the Vale leaves the Ambleside-Keswick main road. Total distance about 8½ miles. Time, about 4½ hours.

Altitude of Passes

Road or footpath	Pass	Location	Height above sea level (ft)
F	Sticks	Ullswater-Thirlspot	2,420
F	Esk Hause	Great Langdale-Wasdale Head	2,386
F	Nan Bield	Mardale-Kentmere	2,100
F	Gatescarth	Mardale-Longsleddale	1,900
F	Black Sail	Wasdale Head-Ennerdale	1,800
F	Sty Head	Wasdale Head-Borrowdale	1,600
F	The Stake	Langdale-Borrowdale	1,570
R	Kirkstone	Windermere-Patterdale	1,500
R	Garburn	Kentmere-Windermere	1,450
F	Scarth Gap	Ennerdale-Buttermere	1,400
R	Hardknott	Cockley Beck-Boot	1,290
R	Wrynose	Little Langdale-Cockley Beck	1,280
R	Honister	Borrowdale-Buttermere	1,176
R	Newlands Hause	Buttermere-Newlands	1,096
R	Whinlatter	Keswick-Cockermouth	1,043
R	Dunmail Raise	Grasmere-Keswick	780

Esk Hause links Wasdale Head with Great Langdale and is perhaps the grandest pass-storming trip in England, taking the cyclist right into the very heart of the highest mountains in the country. Use of the track also takes the cyclist off many miles of roundabout main road. It is preferable to travel from west to east instead of the reverse as the climb up the Sty Head Pass (which is used on the Wasdale Side) is more practicable with a bicycle than the fierce ladder of Rossett Ghyll.

From Wasdale Head take the path past Burnthwaite Guest House which immediately leads to a wild upland valley, up which the Sty Head Pass climbs, at the foot of Great Gable. Lingmell Beck is kept to the right throughout. The Lingmell Crags can be seen on the right, while the chasm of Piers Gill, perhaps the most spectacular in Lakeland, is seen later climbing towards Scafell Pike. The track is stony, and some carrying is needed towards the summit (1,600 ft.), which is reached after two miles. A signboard indicates the way leftwards down Sty Head Gill, but for Esk Hause the way is straight ahead, keeping south of Sty Head Tarn in its hollow. Turn rightwards shortly and then go through a small nick in the fells, crossing and following a beck on the right until it emerges from the western corner of Sprinkling Tarn. The crags of Great End are well seen on the right. Keep in a south-easterly direction beyond the tarn, following its main feeder. The track does not actually cross the main ridge of Esk Hause (between Borrowdale and Eskdale), but continues roughly parallel to it on the north-east, or Borrowdale side. There are a shelter and cairn to the right of the track.

On the descent, maintain the same south-easterly direction (avoiding all temptations to descend down the two valleys on each side of Tongue End), and then go below the outlet from Angle Tarn. There is a sharp rise, and then the summit of Rossett Gill is reached. Thereafter there is a difficult zig-zag drop to the foot of the Stake Pass and the long trench of Mickleden. Total distance about 8 miles. Time, about 6 hours. (By going down the Sty Head Pass, Borrowdale can be reached at Seatoller.)

The **Nan Bield Pass** provides an escape from the head of Mardale, beyond the top of the new Haweswater Reservoir, to

Kentmere, Staveley and Kendal, thus being an alternative to the main road over Shap Fell.

From Bampton (west of Shap village) the new reservoir of Haweswater is approached. Starting at the new dam at the foot of what was formerly a solitary lake, a new, well-surfaced road runs along the eastern side and keeps well above the water. The road ends where the Gatescarth track leaves the Nan Bield footpath, the former going left (see next route, below), and the latter keeping straight on. The valley is grand, with Harter Fell prominent ahead. The track goes to the right of Harter Fell and skirts the north and west sides of a neat tarn called Small Water before climbing sharply to the summit of the pass.

The far side is equally abrupt, and then there is a long, steadier descent well above the eastern side of Kentmere Reservoir, with a lane reached at about 900 ft., and then riding is possible down into Kentmere village. Total distance, 8 miles. Time, 3½ hours.

Extension by the Garburn Pass to Windermere

If the cyclist is not returning to the south after crossing the Nan Bield Pass, he can go westwards into the Lake District proper once again by crossing the Garburn Pass—much cut-up during the war.

The ascent of the Garburn Pass commences at Kentmere Church. First it goes northwards and then bends across a beck and runs westwards, leaving Kentmere Hall down on the left. There is a steep rise to the summit, from which a splendid view of the whole central Lakeland massif, from Coniston Old Man to the Langdale Pikes, can be seen ahead, with the square shape of Great Gable particularly prominent.

On the descent, Windermere can be seen ahead. At a fork opposite a plantation, turn right to join the Kirkstone-Windermere road a little south of Troutbeck. Distance from Kentmere to Troutbeck, 4 miles. Time, 1½ hours.

The **Gatescarth Pass** provides a more direct connection between Haweswater and Kendal than the Nan Bield Pass. On the far side the long descent by road down Longsleddale amply repays the labour of the crossing.

33

Turn sharply left at the far end of the Haweswater road (see Nan Bield Pass description, page 32) and follow a tributary stream closely and steeply to the summit.

On the descent, go down sharply at first to the headwaters of the River Sprint and then keep southwards with the valley, on the right of the stream, with the path becoming a cart-track and improving in surface all the way down to the first farm at Sadgill. From this point a good road runs down the valley to Garnett Bridge (near the main Shap-Kendal road) and into Kendal. Total distance, Mardale to Kendal, 15 miles. Time, 3½ hours.

The **Black Sail Pass** can be used in conjunction with the Scarth Gap Pass (its continuation northwards) to provide a direct route between Wasdale and Buttermere. It is, however, a strenuous journey that might take the greater part of a day. The trip may be broken for a night's stay about halfway at the Black Sail Hut Youth Hostel, the only building, in the desolate country near the source of the River Liza.

The ascent commences beyond the inn at Wasdale Head and goes leftwards, away from the track for Burnthwaite and the Sty Head Pass. For a time the track runs upwards with the Mosedale Beck, keeping to the east side, and then climbs steeply rightwards to a gap in the range which is the Black Sail Pass proper. The valley is hemmed in by lofty hills, and there is no marshy stretch at the summit, as on some passes, but instead a rocky ledge that overlooks the Liza valley, with the Black Sail Hut dwarfed 1,000 ft. below. Across the valley the Scarth Gap track can be seen climbing to the opposite ridge.

On the descent, a beck is soon found, and this is kept on the right to a bridge across the River Liza a few hundred yards below which the Black Sail Hut youth hostel will be gained. Distance, Wasdale to Black Sail Hut, 3½ miles. Time, about 3 hours.

NOTE. A path down the Rivet Liza's north side and then alongside the north side of Ennerdale Water leads in six miles to the Anglers' Inn and Ennerdale Bridge (8 miles). The path turns off the Scarth Gap route a short way west of the hostel, and much of its lower course, especially from near Gillerthwaite Farm, is rideable.

The **Scarth Gap Pass** forms a continuation of the previous trip over the Black Sail Pass, and its views are only a little inferior to those of the latter pass.

From the Black Sail Hut go along the valley floor for less than half a mile. Then turn right, away from the path that continues down the dale, and immediately start to climb in a ladder-like fashion to the lowest nick in the range that separates the head of Ennerdale from the Buttermere Valley.

The descent is at first rough and steep, with the lower part hair-pinning amongst grassy slopes. A bridge leads across the flats at the top of Buttermere and emerges on the Honister-Buttermere road at the sheep farm of Gatesgarth. Distance, Black, Sail Hut to Gatesgarth Farm, 3½ miles. Time, about 2½ hours.

The **Stake Pass** is one of the most useful of the foot passes in the Lake District, linking directly the great scenic centres of Langdale and Borrowdale with a comparatively short and relatively 'easy' pass.

From Middle Fell Place, in Great Langdale, go up the deep hollow of Mickleden, and at a sheepfold turn right, away from the Rossett Gill track, up the west side of a steep beck. This zig-zags towards the top of the climb out of the valley and then crosses the beck, after which it goes over a moraine-filled upland to the summit.

Following a level stretch, the side of the Stake Beck is reached, and then accompanied into Langstrath, a long and straight dale, along the east side of which the rough track proceeds until the river is crossed, whereafter there is a tolerable track down to the hamlet of Stonethwaite and into Borrowdale near Rosthwaite. Distance from Middle Fell Place to Rosthwaite, 7 miles. Time, about 4 hours.

A DAY AWHEEL FROM LITTLE LANGDALE
(From Little Langdale to Little Langdale—38 miles)

Take the road down the valley towards Ambleside, but on joining the Ambleside-Coniston road, close to Colwith Bridge (2), turn right towards Coniston and over the summit. Then, after 2½ miles along the Coniston highway, turn left at Low Yewdale and by **Waterhead** (avoiding Coniston village), where turn right and then left along the eastern side of Coniston Water past **Brantwood**, last home of John Ruskin, to Nibthwaite, at the foot of the lake. This route is preferable to the main west-side road, for it is quieter, more level and closer to the water. Just short of Lowick Bridge turn left, uphill away from River Crake, and down into the hamlet of Oxen Park, where left and through wooded upland valleys to Thwaite Head. Then turn left and by Low Dale Park, Middle Dale Park and High Dale Park, all farms deep in the forests, by a short, steep drop to the shore of **Esthwaite Water**, where sharp right and by Near and Far Sawrey to Windermere Ferry. Follow the shoreline byway northward to High Wray. Turn right here to a bridge and the Coniston-Ambleside road at Clappersgate, just west of Ambleside, and then left with Rivery Brathay to Skelwith Bridge, Colwith Bridge and Little Langdale again.

This round of about 38 miles introduces the cyclist to the quietest corners of southern Lakeland. It is a jaunt that takes seven hours, however, and there are very few places where meals can be obtained, so carry lunch and tea.

THREE DAY-TRIPS FROM KESWICK

1. THE BRANDELHOW ROUND
(From Keswick back to Keswick—12 miles)

No short circuit from Keswick can compare with the Derwentwater and Brandelhow Park round described here. Leave Keswick by the main road running north-westwards, but go straight ahead when, just out of the town, this road forks right. Then around the north end of Derwentwater to **Portinscale**, where turn left and below Swinside Hill (on the right) through woodland. Just short of **Swinside** village turn left downhill and, as the road rises, go left again along a fine terrace road above the lake and into Brandelhow Park. The views behind Derwentwater at Skiddaw and Saddleback are wide and delightful. Continue by Manesty to **Grange** (watch for gates) and the outward route to this point from Keswick described in the main route (page 24).

2. KIRKSTONE AND ULLSWATER
(Keswick to Keswick—47 miles)

Two of the main attractions of the Lake District, the Kirkstone Pass and Ullswater, can be visited in a day's round from Keswick but the route is almost entirely by main road, and is often busy with motor-coach traffic during the summer months. The round can be accomplished, however, with no more than about 10 miles of the main route retraced if the main east-side road by Thirlmere is used.

Leave Keswick by Castlerigg and then through the less interesting upland to **Thirlspot** and the shores of Thirlmere. After the short rise to Dunmail Raise, a two-mile descent follows to near **Grasmere** (the main road skirts it to the east), and on by **Rydal Water** (Wordsworth's home, Rydal Mount, is on the left) through charming lakeside scenery to **Ambleside** (18). Turn left past the church at the northern end of the town and climb with the ledge-road above Stock Gill for three hard miles (called, in part, 'The Struggle'). Some of the middle section is fairly easy, but the final stretch to the Travellers' Rest (1,476 ft.), where the main highway from Windermere to Patterdale (Ullswater) is joined, is steep again.

The summit of the Kirkstone Pass is some 200 yds. beyond the inn, and the surroundings are desolate. The tiny lake far below is **Brothers Water**. Extreme care is needed on the drop to the lake, beyond which the valley and road flatten out as they approach **Patterdale** (27).

Continue alongside Ullswater, second largest of the lakes, noteworthy for its river-like impression because of its three distinct reaches. Beyond Glenridding the road bends rightwards. Three miles from Patterdale leave the cycle near the road forking left and visit **Aira Force**, a graceful fall in an attractive ravine. Return to the fork and signpost and climb leftwards to the village of **Dockwray** and into **Matterdale**, where the quaint church is worthy of inspection. Then follows a fine run down to Troutbeck Station (37), where turn left and by a hilly and follow a relatively featureless road through **Threlkeld** back to Keswick (47).

3. WHINLATTER PASS AND BASSENTHWAITE LAKE

(Keswick to Keswick—25 miles)

A mild, pleasant and quiet round from Keswick is by the Whinlatter Pass to the market town of Cockermouth and back by the west side of Bassenthwaite Lake.

Leave Keswick by Portinscale and pass through the whitewashed village of **Braithwaite**, alpine-looking with its tall buildings and narrow alleys. The zig-zag climb up the Whinlatter Pass is noteworthy for the forestry plantations which in places spoil the view of Bassenthwaite Lake. The road surface is good, and after a two-mile rise to the summit (1,046 ft.) there is a four-mile descent to within three miles of **Cockermouth** (12). In the main street is the birthplace of Wordsworth. The Castle, which is open to visitors, is well situated and dates in part from Roman times.

Leave the town by the road, going east to **Bassenthwaite Lake Station** (17) and along the pretty shore road through forestry lands to Portinscale and Keswick (25).

HILL CLIMBING ON FOOT

The cyclist in the Lake District ought to discard his bicycle whenever he can and climb a hill. Some of the climbs are day-long affairs, while others are merely pleasant evening strolls. In the former category come ascents of mountains like Great Gable or Helvellyn, for which the ordinary light footgear as worn by cyclists is not really suitable; although, if the choice is between climbing in cycling shoes and not climbing at all, the former is to be preferred! During a week's Lakeland holiday the cyclist will probably not wish to climb more than two major hills, and his light shoes, if stoutly shod before leaving home, will serve, provided that the weather is fair.

No expedition afoot into the mountains should be undertaken if the weather is at all misty or rainy. Apart from the fact that one of the objects of mountain climbing, looking at views, is lost if the summit attained is wreathed in cloud, there is always the danger of losing one's way, with serious consequences quite possible. It is the height of selfishness for an inexperienced cyclist to climb a hill, get lost, and then have local farmers (who work hard enough without adding to their worries) and visitors (who are in the district for a holiday, not as part of a search party) to spend hours looking for him.

The walking wheelman should never go on the fells alone, and he should carry (preferably in his saddle-bag, made into a temporary rucksack with cape straps) sufficient food for 20 hours, a watch, a compass and a reliable map, such as 'The Lake District' one-inch sheet of the Ordnance Survey. Cape and sou'wester, matches, a lamp, spare stockings and towel and soap should also go into the bag.

Evening strolls are in a different category. Some of the summits reached during a walk of an hour or two after an evening meal are capable of revealing far more in views than their modest height might suggest. Of this type are Orrest Head, near Windermere, and the Catbells Ridge, on the western side of Derwentwater.

A word in case the cyclist does get lost when on the fells. If caught by nightfall or a mist, the safest plan is to find a hollow, get as comfortable as possible and wait for dawn or for the mist to disperse. This is much less disconcerting than stepping over a precipice—and much less trouble to those who might have to look for him.

The tracks to the summits of most of the mountains are well defined, and their starting points are well established. Many of the ascents can be combined with pass-storming, provided that the bicycle is hidden away from the tracks before being left.

The subsequent descriptions of mountain climbs are meant to be read, in most cases, in conjunction with the section on 'Lakeland Pass-storming for the Cyclist'. In most cases the starting points are places where bicycles can be left under cover and where refreshments can be obtained.

Scafell Pike (3,210 ft.). From Great Langdale (Middle Fell Place). Return distance, 13 miles. Time needed, nine hours.

Follow the footpath north-westwards up Mickleden, and at a sheepfold at the foot of the Stake Pass keep straight ahead up the steep, wall-like ascent of Rossett Ghyll, and then past Angle Tarn to Esk Hause. Follow the cairns south-westwards by the side of Broad Crag along a rough track. The final steep climb of ten minutes is along a narrow ridge with a winding path.

Heights of Principal Lakeland Mountains

	Feet above sea level
Scafell Pike	3,210
Scafell	3,162
Helvellyn	3,118
Skiddaw	3,054
Great End (north-west of Esk Hause)	2,984
Bowfell	2,960
Great Gable	2,949
Pillar	2,927
EskPike	2,903
Fairfield	2,863
Saddleback	2,847
Crinkle Crags	2,816

Highest Summits in Scotland and Wales

Ben Nevis (highest in Britain)	4,406
Snowdon (highest in England and Wales)	3,560

The view takes in a wild and majestic foreground, the lower end of Wastwater (westwards) and part of Derwentwater (north-eastwards), the latter being backed by Skiddaw and Saddleback. The domed head of Great Gable, too, is nearly due north, while a little to the left (or westwards) of Great Gable is Kirkfell and still farther to the north west the Pillar Mountain and Red Pike. Also in this direction are the Solway Firth and the hills of Galloway. In the Irish Sea can be seen the Isle of Man. To the south-east, in the far distance, the flat top of Ingleborough stands but amidst the other summits of the Craven Highlands. In very clear weather Slieve Donard, in County Down, can be seen, just to the north of the Manx Snaefell.

Scafell (3,162 ft.). During a long summer's day the climb to Scafell Pike can be extended profitably to Scafell, with about another 2½ hours of walking there and back from the summit of Scafell Pike.

First drop into the Mickledore chasm and cross its floor to the base of Scafell. Then descend steeply to a grass ledge below the crags and above the screes and next climb the scree track called Lord's Rake. This goes westwards towards Wastwater, first up a gully and by three buttresses of the hill to the top of the cliffs, and so, bearing leftwards, to the summit. The view that Scafell commands of Wastwater is better than the one of the lake as seen from the Pike. On the west and east the crags drop steeply down on Wasdale and Eskdale. Scafell is not a mountain for the beginner, and should not be attempted in bad conditions

Helvellyn (3,118 ft.). From Patterdale, via Striding Edge. Return distance, eight miles. Time, seven hours.

Leave Patterdale by the road up the Grisedale Beck to the northwest of the resort, but shortly branch rightwards and climb the side of the fell to a conspicuous gate some two miles to the west. Go through this and bend leftwards, south of Red Tarn (which is in a hollow on the right), along Striding Edge, an exciting traverse without danger to those with steady heads. The track winds in and out amidst the castellations of the crest of the Edge, and the way to the summit of Helvellyn is unmistakable.

The view comprises Windermere, Coniston and Esthwaite Water to the south and Morecambe Bay beyond them. Ullswater lies to the north-east. Away to the west is the great mountain massif that has Scafell Pike, Great Gable and the Pillar Mountain as its most prominent peaks.

Skiddaw (3,054 ft.). From Keswick. Return distance, eight miles. Time, seven hours return.

Skiddaw is the 'safest' and easiest mountain in the Lake District for the comparative novice at fell-walking.

Leave Keswick by the lane that passes to the right of the station and then take the second lane on the right round the hill called Latrigg. Join another lane (from Applethwaite) and bend rightwards to a point where the woods end. Then swing leftwards and along an unmistakable path, passing first along the slope west of the Whitbeck, and then close to Skiddaw Low Man, and so on to the summit at Skiddaw High Man.

The view northwards across Solway Firth extends from Merrick, in the west, to the hills beyond Moffat, at the head of Annandale. The prominent round hill in the foreground (although across the bay) is Criffel, in Kirkcudbrightshire.

Great Gable (2,949 ft.). From Seathwaite, Borrowdale. Return distance, seven miles. Time, six hours return.

Start from the hamlet of Seathwaite, which is 1¼ miles south-west of Seatoller, at the far end of a short cul-de-sac. Then walk up the Derwent valley between the steep slopes of Glaramara (left) and Base Brown (right), with the precipices of Great End ahead. At Stockley Bridge, cross the left-hand beck and follow the right one steeply up the Sty Head Pass.

From the foot of the Sty Head Tarn leave the pass and turn towards the north-west on the left-hand side of the gully called Aaron Slack. At the head of the depression between Green Gable and Great Gable turn left to the top of the latter mountain.

There is a first-class view from the summit of Great Gable. The whole of Wastwater lies to the south-west, flanked on the left by the Wasdale Screes and on the right by Yewbarrow. The view in this direction includes the sea and the Isle of Man. Scafell and Bowfell can also be seen clearly towards the south and south-east, while in all directions the prospect is most extensive and impressive. Great Gable is perhaps the finest of all Lakeland hills for the cyclist who wishes to get a general idea of the mountains.

Coniston Old Man (2,635 ft.). From Coniston. Time, five hours return. Follow the Church Beck for nearly a mile to the Old Copper Mines, and there bend towards the south-west (crossing the beck that emerges from Levers Water). Go rightwards after half a mile and by the south-east side of Low Water to the summit of the Old Man. The view is an extensive one, ranging from the broad sea through a vista of rich woodlands to the savagery of the Lakeland giants. Coniston Lake, too, makes a pleasing picture below, to the east, although quarry debris greatly mars the mountain.

Saddleback (2,847 ft.). From Threlkeld, 4½ miles west of Keswick. Time, five hours return.

Saddleback, one of the outlying hills of the Lake District, is a fine hill to climb in comparison with its comparatively tame neighbour, Skiddaw. From Threlkeld take the Penrith road for 1½ miles and then follow a path that climbs round a shoulder of the mountain. The southern cliff of the main ridge should be kept on the left and Scales Tarn (in the hollow) on the right. Walk along the several summits, along ridge after ridge. The finest views are towards the south, with the St. John's in the Vale in the foreground, Thirlmere and Derwentwater filling the middle distance at the feet of Helvellyn and the Scafell groups.

The descent can be made by going west from the summit, skirting the cliffs and dropping down a steep round shoulder of the mountain into Threlkeld.

The Highest Inns in England

Name	Location	Altitude
Tan Hill Inn	Yorks (North Riding), between Keld and Kirkby Stephen	1,727 ft.
Cat and Fiddle	Cheshire, between Macclesfield and Buxton	1,690 ft.
Travellers' Rest	Staffs (Flash Bar), between Buxton and Leek	1,534 ft.
Isle of Skye	Yorks (West Riding), between Greenfield and Holmfirth	1,477 ft.
Travellers' Rest	Westmorland	1,476 ft

SOME CENTRES IN THE LAKE DISTRICT

AMBLESIDE (Keswick, 16¼; Kendal, 13) has a central position in the Lake District, although out of sight of Windermere, its nearest lake. The modern church has been criticized as being out of proportion to its surroundings. The adjacent scenery is park-like, but to the north and west the mountains rise. The best short excursion afoot is to Stock Ghyll Force, half a mile east of the town, where the water comes down in two falls which have a total height of 60 ft. The Rothay Valley, to the west side of the town, is worthy of exploration. Ambleside is the best starting place for the Langdale round, taking in Rothay Bridge, Skelwith Bridge, Colwith Force, Little Langdale, Blea Tarn, Dungeon Ghyll, Great Langdale, High Close, Grasmere and so back to Ambleside, a journey of 20 miles that is worth a full day for the leisurely cyclist. (The greater part of the round is included in the Lakeland tour on previous pages.)

CONISTON (Ambleside, 8; Keswick, 23) is delightfully placed at the head of Coniston Lake and the best headquarters for the Lancashire fells at the southern end of Lakeland. **Brantwood**, now the property of the National Trust, about three miles away and on the eastern (opposite) shore of Coniston Water, was the home of John Ruskin, the author and critic, one of the earliest defenders of the countryside. The finest three local excursions are the ascent of Coniston Old Man (see page 42) and the walks to **Tarn Hows** and **Tilberthwaite Gill** (see page 22).

GRASMERE (Ambleside, 4) is a friendly village in the very heart of the country of the Lakeland poets. In the churchyard, close to the River Rothay on the south side, is the grave of William Wordsworth, who died in 1850. The church itself is massive and plain. Grasmere is a fine walking centre, but hardly as good for cycling because of the semi circle of hills to the north. The village lies west of the main Ambleside-Keswick road. Dove Cottage, the home of Wordsworth from 1799 to 1808, is close to the main road, and can be visited without entering Grasmere proper. (Admission charge, 6d.) Amongst the walking routes is that which leads round Grasmere Lake by Red Bank and Loughrigg Terrace, a wholly delightful trip of four miles.

Another is the walk to Easedale Tarn and back, starting from the church and alongside Sour Milk Gill, to the west of the village, on to the tarn itself, a trip of four miles. Yet another is to Tongue Gill, starting from Tongue Gill Beck, along the Keswick road, and taking the Grisedale route towards Helvellyn to a small but picturesque fall. The aqueduct leading from Thirlmere to Manchester passes close by.

Coniston Lake

KENDAL (Lancaster, 21; Preston, 43). The main gateway to the Lake District from the south and the start of the southern ascent of Shap Fell on the main West Coast route to Carlisle and Scotland. The church is 13th century and has five distinct aisles, all of equal length. The castle is chiefly noteworthy for a good view of the southern fells of Lakeland. Good accommodation for cyclists can be found here.

KESWICK (Ambleside, 16¼). The main centre (together with the nearby area) for the northern part of the Lake District. The town is a tourist resort with a busy main street. The parish church is an interesting structure, situated in open country over half a mile northwards of the town, at Crosthwaite. A church has existed here since before the Conquest. Derwentwater is about three-quarters of a mile from the centre of Keswick. The best short walking excursions are to Castle Head, Friar's Crag and Applethwaite. **Castle Head**, the finest local viewpoint, is a wooded height half a mile from

Keswick, to the left of the Borrowdale road. From the top of the hill the whole of Derwentwater can be seen, with the Jaws of Borrowdale and the crags at the far end of the lake. **Friar's Crag** offers the best lake-level view close to Keswick. It is about a mile from the centre of the town, and is reached by the Lake Road. There are facilities for boating here. **Applethwaite**, 2½ miles north of Keswick by road, is an attractive village, and from the lane between it and Millbeck—a quiet alternative to the main road—there is a glorious mountain and lake prospect towards the south, right across the full length of Derwent water and up Borrowdale. In an Applethwaite garden there is a large dulcimer made from sounding stones, out of which a tune can be contrived. The cottage accommodation here is very good. The **Druidical Stones**, 1¾ miles east of Keswick, and reached by Brigham and the old Penrith road, form another walking trip. They are to be seen in a field beyond Castle Lane, in the form of a circle, some of them being over seven feet tall. A longer excursion, well worthwhile, is to the hamlet of Watendlath, five miles from Keswick. The Borrowdale road must be followed for two miles at the end of which a lane leads leftwards. From Ashness Bridge there is a very fine view, and the way on to Watendlath is like a Scottish glen, with grand rock and wooded scenery. The hamlet itself consists of several farmhouses. One of the choicest evening runs from Keswick by bicycle is through the Newlands Valley by Portinscale, Swinside, Stair and as far as Keskadale and back.

KIRKBY LONSDALE (Kendal, 12½); A romantic town on a hill above the river Lune. The town and the picturesque Devil's Bridge are now by-passed by a modern road and a new bridge, but the discerning cycle tourist should take the old road to the right when approaching from the Bradford and Settle direction, cross the Devil's Bridge and enter Kirkby Lonsdale. Ruskin praised the view of valley, river and mountain seen from the churchyard.

PENRITH (Kendal, 27; Carlisle, 18). An old town on the main road (A6) from Kendal to Carlisle, with narrow streets and an historic air. The best local viewpoint is Penrith Beacon (937 ft.) closed during war and now reopened. At Clifton, 2½ miles south, is the scene of the last battle on English soil, between the retreating forces of Prince Charles Edward and the pursuing English.

Cycling in the Lake District today

As Harold Briercliffe wrote this cycle route guide in 1947, many of the roads he mentions are not suitable for cycling today. Suggested alternative cycle routes, from Sustrans, which are in the same location as Harold's original route are listed below. To devise your own detailed route and map in the region, go to www.sustrans.org.uk for online mapping, free iphone and android apps.

The Lake District is home to the beginning of two of the National Cycle Network's most popular routes; the **Sea to Sea route** and **Hadrian's Cycleway**. As with many routes you reap the greatest rewards when your legs endure the most punishment. This is particularly true of the Lake District, with stunning views and countryside to feast on when you climb its many slopes.

National Cycle Route 72 runs up the Cumbrian coast towards Carlisle before heading east to Tynemouth. But it is **National Cycle Route 71** that passes through the Lake District with two spurs beginning the famous **Sea to Sea Cycle Route** (from Workington to Penrith it is 46 miles or 53 miles if you take the spur from Whitehaven).

Riding from Workington you get to cross the stunning new bridge over the River Derwent and have a gentler climb to the Lake District National Park. The more spectacular Whitehaven spur guides you past the shimmering Loweswater Lake, which is surrounded by lush green hills and forests, before you begin the second tougher climb up to Whinlatter Pass.

The two strands of National Route 71 join together just before the beautiful market town of **Keswick,** which has become the tourist capital of the north lakes and is a delightful place to stop. Before joining the stunning converted railway path to **Threlkeld** on the way to **Penrith**, the **Castlerigg Stone Circle** is well worth a visit and just a short detour from the Sea to Sea Route.

Useful maps and books (available from www.sustransshop.co.uk)*: Sea to Sea Cycle Route Map; Hadrian's Cycleway Map; The Ultimate C2C Guide; The C2C Cycle Route (Cicerone Guides); Coast to Coast Cycle Routes; Ordnance Survey Tour Map – Lake District; Off-road Trails & Quiet Lanes: Cycling in the Lake District & Yorkshire Dales.*

Whatever the Mileage

the Super Club will get you there

The Super Club (illustrated below) is a superb example of how completely Elswick and Hopper cycles have returned to traditional standards. Many complimentary letters are continually being received from enthusiastic owners praising the beautiful finish of our cycles. Excellent though our models now are, we are persistently and painstakingly devoting all our technical skill to even greater progress in design.

Elswick & Hopper *Cycles*

ELSWICK HOPPER CYCLE & MOTOR CO. LTD., BARTON-ON-HUMBER, LINCOLNSHIRE

PART II

THE YORKSHIRE DALES

INTRODUCTION

THE dales and moors of the West and North Ridings of Yorkshire form a compact and diversified touring area that is almost ideal for cycle touring. Unlike the Lake District, where the main valleys form radials like the spokes of a wheel from the central mountain mass, the Yorkshire Dales are, in the main, laid out in a regular series, southwards from Teesdale (shared with the county of Durham to the north) to Airedale, the general direction of the valleys being from their heads in the north-west amongst the high fells south-east towards the levels of the Yorkshire Ouse.

Scenically the Dales vary in their characteristics. The most northerly of the all-Yorkshire valleys, Swaledale, from Keld to Reeth, for instance, is a true mountain cleft, with its river running swiftly between steep valley sides; while its neighbour, Wensleydale, to the south, is mostly wide and graceful in contrast, even as far up the valley as Hawes, itself a bleak little centre that is more important as a road junction than for any intrinsic interest. Again, Teesdale, to the north of Swaledale, is rich in parks and woodlands between Barnard Castle and Middleton, but above the latter place the mountainous type of scenery prevails, reaching its most dramatic at impressive **High Force**, one of the grandest waterfalls in Britain. Less accessible and more of a cataract is **Cauldron Snout**, where the Tees tumbles out of the bog-lands of the highest stretch of country in the Pennines.

Airedale starts with a sparkling river about Malham, where **The Craven Fault**, a limestone dislocation that stretches across from Upper Wharfedale to near Kirkby Lonsdale, provides the most spectacular cliff scenery in northern England at **Malham Cove** and **Gordale Scar**. After a gentle course through green upland, the River Aire becomes polluted below Skipton and Keighley.

Wharfedale, between Wensleydale and Airedale, is perhaps the dale with most variety, from the bare, rocky hills of its source down to the sophistications of Ilkley. The richest part of the dale is between the latter place—a resort and almost a suburb of Bradford and Leeds—and Grassington, including Bolton Abbey and the deep channel in the river bed called **The Strid**, where the breadth of the Wharfe is narrowed to four feet after being ten times as wide a few yards away.

To the west and northwest of the regular series of dales lie Ribblesdale and Dentdale, with rivers flowing eventually into the Irish Sea. Ribblesdale is remarkable (as are parts of Upper Wharfedale) for the little limestone gorges of the tributaries and the caves and potholes that abound close to it. Few of these 'sights' are commercialized, and perhaps the most remarkable of them all, the 200-ft. hole of **Alum Pot**, near Selside, is within a short walk of the main valley road. There are waterfalls, too, in the valley, the finest on the Ribble itself being at Stainforth, where there is also a 200-year-old packhorse bridge across the river that is now in the safe keeping of the National Trust.

Dentdale is different from the rest of the dales. It is short and its sides are steep, so that its river, the Yorkshire Dee, and its tributaries flow swiftly over slabs of rock, forming here and there waterfalls and 'strids' (rocky chasms so called from the Anglo-Saxon word *stryth*, meaning tumult). The quaint dale capital of **Dent**, with its kinked main street and cobbles, together with a church that looks like a fortress, is perhaps the most distinctive village in all the Dales.

Rather out of the run of the Dales system is the valley of the Nidd, that becomes interesting above the steep streets of Pateley Bridge, although marred by reservoir works at Middlesmoor and lacking a good road outlet at its head. Potholes are to be found in Nidderdale, too, while its highest village, Middlesmoor, on a neb of land, has stone houses which are full of character. The village is close to the narrow, rocky gorge of **How Stean**, the latter being worth a visit to Nidderdale on its own account.

The subsidiary dales are also interesting. Two becks at **Ingleton**, west of Ribblesdale, are commercialized, but well worth seeing, while above one of them a lonely, open valley goes over into brief but romantic Deepdale, that drops down on Dentdale. A tributary of the Wharfe, the River Skirfare, runs through a grey-green valley, passing the hamlet of Litton (giving the name of Littondale to the valley) and the bowers of Arncliffe, eventually joining the River Wharfe close to the overhanging limestone cliff of **Kilnsey Crag**. Other notable side-valleys are Mallerstang (in Westmorland, but close to the Yorkshire dales system), pastoral Bishopdale and the remote cul-de-sac of Waldendale.

The Yorkshire Dales yield some of the best cycling in Britain, There are nearly always two roads up each valley, giving alternative routes, at the times of heavy motor traffic; while almost every valley has an outlet head into the neighbouring dales. Thus many tours of the Yorkshire Dales can be planned to avoid the repetition so common in the Lake District and the Highlands of Scotland.

The characteristic fell and dale country of West and North Yorkshire is unmistakable. There is little level land even on the floor of the dales, and both valley-bottom and climbing hillsides are cut up into innumerable holdings by the stone walls, sometimes straight and often wriggling, which so surprise the newcomer. Mostly the dales are given over to sheep farming, and everywhere the tourist will see these sturdy animals. The many small stone barns that dot the hillsides are stores for winter fodder, while the enclosures close to streams and rivers are dipping places. The houses and farms of the Dales are often old and always built from local stone, and while strictly utilitarian in intention, are frequently most picturesque. Thwaite and Muker, in Swaledale, are as ugly in a sense as their Norse-names, but their very grimness and strength grows on the lover of the Dales until at last he comes to realize how much they are in harmony with their wild mountain setting. The loveliest or prettiest village in the Dales is, as always, a matter of opinion. The writer would give **Clapham**, on the main Settle-Ingleton road, high marks, and **Burnsall**, on the banks of the Wharfe, is bonny, too. Wensley, Arncliffe, Malham and Masham are all attractive, amongst many others, in their own particular ways; but the writer must confess that his favourite village is **Keld**, in Upper Swaledale, where old houses cluster in a hollow off the road and hang above the clear hill stream as it takes the plunge through the trees at **Kisdon Force**.

In the tours that follow, the stopping places are small centres that provide accommodation for the bed-and-breakfast traveller or for the camper. In all cases there are also youth hostels in the villages or not far away.

In conclusion, a word about accommodation would not be out of place. Most of the catering places in the stopping-places indicated are of a modest nature, of the cottage or farmhouse type which appeals to the cyclist. The fare provided is good and homely. Prices vary, but even at present rates the average cost of bed and breakfast at Dales farms should not be more than 6s.

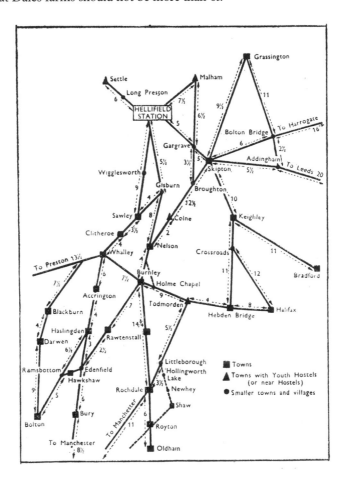

Approaches to Hellifield for the Yorkshire Dales.
(Diagram not to scale)

APPROACHES

Hellifield, on the L.M.S. main line (former Midland), from London (St. Pancras) to Glasgow (St. Enoch), is undoubtedly the handiest starting place for a tour of the Yorkshire Dales (see map opposite). It is directly linked thus with the two largest cities in the country, and also with Leeds, Bradford, Edinburgh, Manchester, Liverpool, Bristol, Derby, Birmingham, Leicester and other centres. Of all the large cities, Newcastle is the only one which is not handy for Hellifield. by rail. The Tyneside wheelman could, however, join the touring routes given in the following pages at a more northerly point, at Barnard Castle or Richmond, for instance.

The tourist from the south who prefers to travel all the way by road will find that a route by the Great North Road to Wetherby and then by Collingham, Pool, Otley, Ilkley, Addingham, Skipton and Gargrave will take him to Hellifield without the complication of crossing the Lancashire and West Riding industrial belts. (If making for Malham, he can turn off at Gargrave without going into Hellifield.) From Birmingham and the south-west the smoothest and least industrialized approach is by Stafford, Newcastle-under-Lyme, Holmes Chapel, Mere Corner, Warrington, Wigan, Preston, Whalley, Clitheroe and Gisburn. Forbidding as some parts of this route may be, the roads are far smoother than they were twenty years ago and no large cities are entered.

From the Manchester district, a roundabout but smoother and more interesting approach than the orthodox one by Bury and Whalley is by Failsworth, along the new road called The Broadway, through Shaw and Newhey, then turning right in Milnrow and by Hollingworth Lake, Littleborough, Todmorden, Holme Chapel, where right, off the Burnley road, and by Mereclough to a by-pass road where right, and so to the Burnley-Nelson road, where right again for Nelson, Barrowford, Gisburn and Hellifield.

Bradford wheelmen can best approach Hellifield by way of Keighley, Skipton and Gargrave; while Leeds riders can join the above route at Skipton after travelling by Guiseley, Ilkley and Addingham, and going over the long climb by Draughton to Skipton.

A FOUR-DAY TOUR OF 113 MILES

Hellifield Station: Down the station approach, then left to Hellifield (no interest, except peel tower to the south), left in village and left again (leaving the main Skipton road) along a pleasant and hilly lane by the old-world village of Otterburn and some steeper gradients into **Airton** (4 miles), which has a green and 17th century houses. Left at the crossroads into **Kirkby Malham**, a picturesque hamlet, with a church register that has a signature reputed to be that of Oliver Cromwell. The undulating highway continues northwards towards Malham. From the top of the descent into the village there is a fine view of the 300-ft. limestone cliff of Malham Cove, a fitting centrepiece to grey hills diversified by criss-crossing walls and belts of mountain ash. And so into Malham (7½).

Malham is a scattered hamlet on the Craven Fault, close to two remarkable limestone 'sights,' Malham Cove and Gordale Scar. This is the end of normal road travelling, but there are hilly and narrow outlets to the north-west and north-east. A useful first halting-place for tourists travelling by day trains from London, Malham can be reached by tea-time, leaving the evening for exploring the district afoot.

Leave Malham by the climbing lane west of Malham Cove. Go by Malham Tarn, a featureless sheet of water on a clay bed amidst the otherwise porous limestone outcrops. (Charles Kingsley wrote *The Water Babies* here.) Bend rightwards round the head of the Tarn and by Darnbrook House, down the steep, rough descent into **Arncliffe**. There are some beautiful woods and fine cliff terraces along the sides of Littondale, an inn and an interesting 15th century church (16½ from Hellifield).

Follow the River Skirfare towards the south-east. There are two roads, of which the one to the east is the more interesting. It runs via the hamlet of Hawkswick to Kilnsey, where a 170-ft. crag overhangs the road. Try throwing a stone at the crag from the road. It has been hit, but very rarely. Retrace your route for nearly a mile, then right towards Kettlewell—entered after a fine sweep down from a wooded, terrace—to cross a stone bridge.

Kettlewell (23½), a typical Dales village at the mouth of a tributary of the Wharfe, is worth exploring on foot. The road up this side valley leads by the steep climb of Park Rash, over into Coverdale and Wensleydale, an attractive route, adventurous in winter.

Continuing up Wharfedale, the next village is **Starbotton**, a former metal-mining centre, but now a picturesque group of cottages and farms enclosing the main dales road at the foot of some fine limestone crags. Beyond it is the friendly hamlet of **Buckden** (27½).

Here the road forks, the left-hand branch going into the green and grey loveliness of Langstrothdale. It is worthwhile climbing Langstrothdale as far as Oughtershaw and returning to Buckden (38). In Langstrothdale see tiny Hubberholme Church, dating from the 13th century, and the picturesque hamlets of Yockenthwaite, Deepdale and Oughtershaw, where there is an ancient hall.

On returning to Buckden, climb steeply to Cray, where the falls below the inn are very pretty. Just short of the summit of the road into Bishopdale turn left along a stony and grass-grown lane over Kidstones Fell to the Stake Pass (1,832 ft.), where a fine prospect across Wensleydale to the fells beyond is obtained. A long and rough descent leads to a close view of **Semerwater**, one of Yorkshire's few lakes. Turn left around the foot of the lake (where there are sites for camping) to Countersett. From Stalling Busk village above Semerwater (below the descent from The Stake Pass), it is possible to approach Parker Gill Force, a small but picturesque waterfall. From Countersett an up-and-down lane leads to **Bainbridge** (48½), a pleasant centre on the main Wensleydale road.

NOTE. Riders who like to feel a smooth road under their wheels can cut out the Stake Pass by continuing from Oughtershaw and across Fleet Moss (1,900 ft.), and then down a steep drop (care needed at the start, and towards the finish—beware gates) into Gayle, Hawes and Bainbridge (about 7 miles farther).

Cross the Yore (the river of Wensleydale) into Askrigg (50). Proceed down the dale on the north-side road past fortified Nappa Hall, to Redmire (57). Go off the road to Bolton Castle, a fortress with chequered history, which is built at a salient point in Wensleydale. Climb over a hill road (1,550 ft.) to Grinton, and cross the River Swale into **Reeth** (63), a village sited around a large, tilted green.

Proceed westwards up narrow Swaledale along the swinging and undulating road on the north side of the river, by Feetham, Low Row and **Gunnerside** (69), all small villages set amidst pastoral scenes.

Cross the slanting bridge across the Swale, and then by **Muker** and **Thwaite**, climbing away from the course of the river (hidden on the right in a hollow behind Kisdon Hill) and by Angram into **Keld** (76). (See page 64.) The village, which lies in a dip to the right of the road, is a good centre for exploring the district. Tan Hill Inn, the highest in England (1,727 ft.) is six miles to the north, and the trip to it and back to Keld is a pleasant evening's run.

Retrace the road by Angram to Thwaite. Turn right beyond the latter and walk up the steep **Buttertubs Pass** between the hills of Lovely Seat and Great Shunner Fell. The 'buttertubs' are deep, mossy, limestone potholes on both sides of the road, and should be examined. It is a sharp, steep climb to the summit (1,726 ft.), from which there is a distant view of Ingleborough, some 16 miles southwards. Caution is needed on the descent. (There is a gate in the middle of a steep pitch near a quarry.) At the T-junction turn right to the George and Dragon Inn for permission (small charge) to view **Hardraw Scaur**, where a waterfall topples about 75 ft. down the middle of a fine circular amphitheatre. The path leads *behind* the fall. Then return to the foot of Buttertubs Pass and then across water meadows to the bleak town of **Hawes** (85). Turn left at the western end of Hawes and over the hill into Widdale, a wild, treeless valley, where the road climbs steadily to the moorland summit at Newby Head Inn (1,421 ft.). On the descent, Ingleborough (2,373 ft), like a beheaded cone, will be seen ahead; the bulky hill to the north-west is Whernside (2,414 ft.). Short of Ribblehead Station, turn sharp left and then alongside the infant River Ribble down a walled lane with a good surface. Just before the railway is crossed by a bridge, a farm track leads left to Ingman Lodge and the foot of **Ling Gill**, a steep, rocky chasm, worth exploring afoot (time needed from the road and back, 2½ hours). At the head of the small village of Selside, a track leads right to **Alum Pot Hole**, 250 ft. deep, walled-in, and well worth a visit (time needed, one hour from Selside and back). Continuing down Ribblesdale, the first large village is straggling **Horton** (102). The church, on the left after crossing the river, has a noteworthy Norman porch. The prominent hill to east is Pen-y-ghent (2,273 ft.).

Pass close to the hamlet of Helwith Bridge and into **Stainforth** (106).

On Cowside Beck, to the east of the village, is Catterick Force, with two falls of 25 ft. each. Closer, on the River Ribble, to the west of Stainforth, is **Stainforth Fosse**, approached by a graceful one-arch bridge that is now in the hands of the National Trust. The Fosse can be seen readily from the west side of the river, but visitors should beware of the slipperiness of the limestone above the fall and the deep pool below and not approach too closely. Fatal accidents have occurred at this point. From Stainforth village it is a run of a little more than two miles into **Settle** (108). The green dome seen on the right approaching Settle belongs to the Giggleswick Grammar School. (See page 66.)

NOTE. A road runs westwards from Settle by the pretty village of Clapham and Clapham Common (there is even a Clapham Junction on the railway) to Ingleton, and its waterfalls, which though well advertised, should certainly be seen. From Settle the final miles run eastwards by the village of **Long Preston** and Hellifield.

The tour detailed above, while by no means comprehensive, is representative of all kinds of Yorkshire Dales scenery, except for the more popular types to be found in the lower parts of the valleys. While it omits such places as Bolton Abbey and Richmond, it threads the quieter upper portions of the main dales, and thus introduces the newcomer to the district to the remoter villages, and hill crossings that are especially dear to the wheelman. The halting places at Malham, Askrigg and Keld are all well provided with accommodation, including youth hostels, and the cycle-camper will find in the district many unfrequented streamside sites which can hardly be bettered anywhere in the country.

The round, while short in mileage, is hard and hilly in parts, and would repay even a five-day or longer holiday. The strenuous mile-eater could probably get inside it within three days, but he would miss many of the sights and side excursions that are the very cream of cycle touring. The five-day man could follow the round in reverse, starting at Settle and staying around Stainforth (where there is a youth hostel) or Langcliffe for the first night, going on afterwards to Keld, Askrigg and Malham for his other overnight halts.

A NINE-DAY TOUR IN THE DALES

MIDDLE WHARFEDALE
(Kettlewell to Kettlewell—34 miles)

Using the 3½-day tour as the basis, an eight- or nine-day tour of 304 miles can be arranged to bring in Bolton Abbey and the Strid, Nidderdale, Teesdale, Dentdale and Ingleton. A little repetition would be necessary here and there, but with advance planning, five day rounds from points on the skeleton 3½-day tour could give a full holiday in the Dales.

The first stage of this tour is from Hellifield to Malham, Arncliffe and Kettlewell, as in the first tour. With Kettlewell as the base, two day jaunts could be planned as follows (mileages are for day trips only and *not* cumulative from day to day):—

From **Kettlewell** proceed down the east (and quietest) side of the River Wharfe, to the charming village of Conistone, and still southward through Grass Wood past Ghaistrills (a small "strid", where the Wharfe is only three feet wide) into the small town of **Grassington** (5½ miles from Kettlewell). The countryside becomes more wooded through Hebden, giving a fine view of Burnsall village on the opposite bank, and Hartington and **Appletreewick**, beyond which, to the left side of the road, is **Trailers Gill**, a cleft in the limestone some 500 ft. deep and only a few yards wide.

Just before the main road drops to ancient Barden Bridge, a lane swings left and leads to a gated field road above the Wharfe. Opposite, on the far side of the river, are the ruins of Barden Tower, a stronghold of the Clifford family. This field road gives way to an enchanting run through glorious woodland. A mile after deserting the main road, leave your bicycles in the wood and follow the riverside footpath to **The Strid**. The Wharfe is only a yard or two wide for about fifty yards, but the rock is slippery and treacherous, and there have been several fatalities—so don't jump!

The lane on the eastern side of the river continues pretty by Friar Stones and Storiths to Beamsley Hospital (alms houses). Here the way is right to **Bolton Bridge** (17 from Kettlewell). The miles from Barden Bridge are amongst the most delightful in the Dales. A little less than a mile north of Bolton Bridge is the 'Hole in the Wall' that leads to **Bolton Abbey**. The route back to Kettlewell is along the west side of Wharfedale. The bicycles can be left at the 'Hole' (which is literally that), and the 12th century Bolton Abbey, built on one of the finest sites in the Kingdom, can be visited. The main west-side road continues by the Cavendish Fountain, and then, well above the romantic riverside, to Barden Tower, which lies close to the road. Continue up the dale to the charming village of **Burnsall**, close to the river and athwart the road. Hidden away just west of the road is the village of Thorpe, which is well worth diverging slightly to see. Then come the outskirts of Linton and Threshfield in quick succession, and the dale narrows again approaching Kilnsey and its crag and continues to grow wilder until **Kettlewell** is reached again. Total mileage for the day, Kettlewell to Kettlewell, 34—full of interest throughout.

TO NIDDERDALE AND BACK
(Kettlewell to Kettlewell—40 miles)

A further extension, again using Kettlewell as a base, brings in Park Rash, the lonely crossing to Coverdale and the rough climb and descent to the reservoirs at the head of Nidderdale.

Leave **Kettlewell** by the road on the north-west side of the beck that flows through the village. For a mile and a half this winds and undulates, and then climbs sharply up the hill once famous as a testing ground for motor vehicles—**Park Rash**. The long shoulder of the hill seen on the right from the summit is Whernside (2,310 ft.), not to be confused with Whernside, north-west of Ribblehead. Ahead is Little Whernside (1,984 ft.). The road summit is 1,652 ft. above sea level, and beyond it is a steep descent, which eases after crossing the infant River Cover to the north side of the dale. Human habitations appear again at Woodale (8 miles from Kettlewell) and Bradley, but near

Arkleside Steadings take the road rightwards across the bridge, through Arkleside and immediately uphill for nearly two miles to the summit (over 1,700 ft.) on a rough, neglected road. The descent also is rough and in parts unrideable, but the views obtained of Upper Nidderdale are splendid. Cross the foot of Scar House Reservoir to the reservoir road and the railway lines on the south side of Nidderdale. Follow the course of the river downwards, and soon after a sharp right-angled turn in the valley towards the south, look out for **Manchester Hole** and **Goyden Pot**. The depleted River Nidd disappears into the former, while exploration of the passage can be undertaken for a *short* distance. The subterranean rumblings signify the course of the buried river. The most remarkable Nidderdale scene is to be found about two miles ahead, up the tributary valley of **How Stean Beck**, about half a mile above the village of Lofthouse (15 miles from Kettlewell). There is a small admission charge. Access is given to a long, steep-sided crack in the rock, through which a path has been made. The rocks overhead nearly meet at times, and there is a wealth of ferns and shrubs. It is worthwhile extending the walk at the head of this gill to the grandly situated village of **Middlesmoor**, almost 1,000 ft. above sea-level and with a commanding view down the valley. From the village of Lofthouse, a better road continues alongside the tank of water that is the Gouthwaite Reservoir (owned by the Bradford Corporation, like those higher up the valley), first passing Ramsgill, notorious as the birthplace of Eugene Aram, the murderer. **Pateley Bridge** (22), the first large place since Kettlewell, is a typical Pennine townlet of stone, built on a slope on the east side of Nidderdale. Take the steep climb westwards up Greenhow Hill to Greenhow, and then by Stump Cross Cave (small charge), and so back to Wharfedale again, and by Hebden and Grassington to Conistone and Kettle well. (Total mileage for a very hilly and interesting day, 40, Kettlewell to Kettlewell.)

TAN HILL AND TEESDALE
(Keld to Keld—92 miles)

Using **Keld** as a base, a long day can bring in Tan Hill, Brough, Barnard Castle and Teesdale, including High Force and Cauldron

Snout. Go north from Keld to West Stonesdale and up to the open, moorland at Tan Hill Inn (where light refreshments can be obtained), the highest in England (1,727 ft.). After a run across unfenced upland, with distant views of the Lakeland peaks in the west and the long line of high hills to the north that includes Cross Fell, the monarch of the Pennines, there is an awkward descent by Barras Station, and then the road runs across the rich sandstone of the Eden Valley to the small market town of **Brough** (14).

Climb steadily eastwards for 7½ miles to the summit of Bowes Moor, noting on the right Rey Cross, probably a boundary stone, and then go easily downhill into **Bowes**. The first house on the right is regarded as the original of Dotheboys Hall in *Nicholas Nickleby*. Continue along what was once a straight Roman road, to beyond Rokeby, where left, and alongside the River Tees, by Egglestone Abbey, into Barnard Castle. (A short cut from Bowes misses the Teesside scenery.) (Distance from Keld to Barnard Castle, 32 miles.)

Barnard Castle is an old town on a slant above a picturesque bridge over the River Tees, and was formerly famous for its cycling meet.

The Norman doorway to the restored parish church is worth seeing and also the King's Head Inn, where Dickens stayed when writing *Nicholas Nickleby*. The Castle, which dates from the twelfth century, lies between the main street and the river, and can be reached through the yard of the King's Head.

Continue up Teesdale to Lartington, Cotherstone, Romaldkirk and **Middleton-in-Teesdale** (43), The valley is much narrower and wilder hereabouts, and beyond the village of Newbiggin listen for the roar of **High Force**, a sheer fall of 40 ft. between perpendicular rocks, and the greatest waterfall of its kind in Britain. Walk down to its foot by the path opposite the hotel. Regaining the road, continue to Langdon Beck (50), and if time permits go by the rough moorland road first west and then southwards to **Cauldron Snout**, a succession of cataracts through a narrow defile. Above the Snout, in a shallow part of the moorland, the Tees spreads into a long, snaky series of pools called 'The Weel'. The trip to and from Cauldron Snout from Langdon Beck takes about two hours, the total distance being about six miles of hard riding and walking. (Langdon Beck second time, 56 miles.)

The return to Keld is shorter than the outward run, leading from **Middleton-in-Teesdale** (63) over fine moorland by the solitary district of Grains o' the Beck to **Brough** again (78), and then to the town of **Kirkby Stephen** (82), where you should turn left by Nateby and across more solitary places to Hollow Mill Cross (over 1,500 ft.), and by a gated road (caution after dark) to the outward route at Park House, near West Stonesdale, and so to Keld. (Total distance, Keld to Keld, 92 miles.)

This is a long and strenuous day's journey, and it would be advisable for the normal rider to break it with a night's stay at **Middleton-in-Teesdale** or **Newbiggin**, where there is accommodation, or **Langdon Beck**, where there is also a youth hostel.

DENTDALE AND SEDBERGH
(Keld to Hellifield—62 miles)

A further extension, bringing in the attractive country in Dentdale and the country around Sedbergh, on the western side of the Yorkshire Dales, is well worth doing.

For this, cross the Buttertubs Pass from **Keld** and **Muker** to **Hawes** (as in the basic 3½-day route). Instead of going up Widdale, turn right for Moorcock Inn (14 from Keld), where turn left and later down Garsdale (interesting but scenically inferior to Swaledale) to Sedbergh (25). The narrow streets of this old town stand beneath the shapely green forms of the Howgill Fells. Its church is partly Norman, and the town is famous for its public school.

The outstanding natural feature close to Sedbergh is **Cautley Spout**. To reach this waterfall, retrace your route to the fork near the bridge across the River Rawthey, and there turn left to Cautley Beck Inn. Leave the bicycles here and walk up the valley to the Spout, set below a fine amphitheatre of crags and hills. Cautley Spout is four miles from Sedbergh. (Sedbergh, second time, 33 miles.)

Make your way out of Sedbergh, past the Grammar School, and

travel up Dentdale, which is perhaps the finest of the smaller dales, a pastoral hollow between steep valley sides. Dent (39), the 'capital' of the dale, is suggested as a halting-place for the night. Cobbled streets and quaint corners mark the village off as a true mountain retreat. A unique fountain memorial in Shap granite to Adam Sedgwick, the geologist, is a noteworthy feature. There is a youth hostel at Cowgill, near Lea Yeat.

Continue next day up Dentdale by Lea Yeat, noticing the waterfalls, strids and other fine scenic displays provided by the River Dee, which here runs close to the road. There is a steep climb at the head of the dale to open moorland, with the road reaching the Hawes-Ribblehead road as in basic route. (Distance, Keld to Hellifield by this route, 62 miles.)

CENTRES FOR HOLIDAYS OR WEEK-ENDS

There are many small towns and hill-country villages in the Dales that serve admirably as centres or bases for touring. Some of the best of them are described in the subsequent pages, and the information regarding them should be read in conjunction with the descriptions of tours. Most of the places described here are within week-ending range of the North Lancashire, West Riding and Teesside towns. Bed-and-breakfast, camping and youth-hostel facilities will be found at or near all the centres given.

ASKRIGG (Hawes, 6). A grey village on the north side of the River Yore, the stream of Wensleydale. The principal feature of the village is an old Tudor Hall. On Mill Gill Beck, half a mile from Askrigg, are two falls, at Mill Gill and Whitwell. An evening cycle run of six miles is eastwards by Bainbridge (or by a parallel by-road on the north side of the valley) to Aysgarth Falls, above and below a fine bridge across the Yore. The main falls are below the bridge (about ⅛ mile), a succession of cascades over horizontal ledges between woody banks. Another short cycling trip is to Semerwater, a sparkling gem amidst the fells.

DENT (six miles east of Sedbergh). A fortress-like village on the floor of a secluded valley. An attractive run is up Deepdale to White Shaw Moss (handy for the ascent of Whern-side, the highest mountain in the West Riding), returning to Dent, or continuing to

Ingleton (10½ miles from Dent). A really rough route leads from Lea Yeat, four miles above Dent, to Hawes Junction, over Shaking Moss. From Gawthrop, below Dent, there is a steep rise to over 1,000 ft., and then a long descent through a fine upland valley to Barbon, in Lunedale, which is a 'shortcut' route to Morecambe or Furness. There is a youth hostel at Cow Gill, above Dent.

INGLETON (Settle, 11; Hellifield, 17) is the best headquarters for exploring the waterfalls of the **Thornton** and **Ingleton Becks**. A notice, 'This way to the scenery', makes the route from Ingleton obvious and a small charge is made to view the falls. The full round of nearly five miles takes just over two hours walking, which is enough for a morning or a summer's evening. Thornton Foss, situated high on the beck of that name, is the best fall of the series. **Ingleborough**, which, although flat-topped, is the shapeliest of West Yorkshire mountains, can be ascended and descended in about 3½ hours. The usual route starts nearly half a mile along the Hawes road, then by Crina Bottom and up the final climb. The summit (2,373 ft.) is almost a mile in circumference and nearly flat. The view to the northwest embraces the Lakeland summits, including Scafell Pike and Scafell.

Another excursion, this time awheel, is to **Weathercote Cave** and back (4 miles). This cave is to the left of the Ribblehead and Hawes road at Chapel-le-Dale. A stream, after an underground course, bursts out of the rock face and falls 70 ft. into a basin.

KELD (nine miles north of Hawes) is a small hamlet in a hollow close to the River Swale. The Cat-Hole Inn stands closer to the main road. Its name is said to be derived from the fact that it was built to 'catch' the custom of the herdsmen driving their animals across the border. The Swale, flowing through open fells above Keld, plunges below the village over **Kisdon Force**, a double fall amidst crag and wood, into a fine gorge that is worth following southwards towards Muker by the river path (entered by a gate on the right at the foot of Keld's cul-de-sac of a 'main street').

KETTLEWELL (Skipton, 16; Hawes, 17) is a quiet, grey village in Upper Wharfedale, and a convenient centre for excursions afoot and awheel. A most interesting walk is to Arncliffe (3 miles), by bridge over the River Wharfe and up the path under a limestone crag, and so over a ridge (with fine views up Wharfedale) at 1,550 ft., and into the village of Arncliffe, situated in a charming spot in Littondale.

MALHAM (7½ miles north-east of Hellifield and 12 miles north-west of Skipton) is a bright, attractive village at the head of Airedale. Busy on summer week-ends but quiet during the week, it is the best centre for exploring the scenery of the Craven Fault, the showpiece of which is **Gordale Scar**, one mile east of village. (See Plate VII.) To visit the Scar, walk along the lane climbing out of Malham and then down a steep hill (at the foot, on the right, is Janet's Fosse, a small fall in a bowery setting) to Gordale Farm, where the path leads through a farmyard to the Scar, a deep cleft between steep limestone cliffs. An obvious climb up past a fossilized tree to the left of the waterfall leads to the moorland above, whence a rough, unpathed walk westwards of less than an hour leads to the head of Malham Cove.

Buttertubs Pass, Hawes

The Cove is reached more easily by going north from the village. It is really a 300-ft. cliff, from the foot of which issues a stream which forms one of the headwaters of the River Aire. Farther north still is the somewhat featureless Malham Tarn, one of the few lakes in Yorkshire.

Other possible cycling excursions lead south by the main road to

Kirkby Malham and then west to Scaleber Force and Settle; or east over grass-grown Mastiles Lane to Kilnsey Crag. These excursions, though quite worthwhile, are of secondary importance in comparison with the others mentioned here.

SETTLE (Hellifield, 6), which lies in Ribblesdale, at the foot of the limestone crags of Castleberg, is a very good centre. Well worth a visit are Victoria Cave, two miles north-east, noted for finds of prehistoric animals; Scaleber Force, on the steep Kirkby Malham road; the 'Ebbing and Flowing Well,' which lies behind Giggleswick and below the long line of Giggleswick Scar, in a grove to the north side of main Ingleton and Kendal road. There is a youth hostel at Stainforth, 2½ miles north.

Cycling in the Yorkshire Dales today

As Harold Briercliffe wrote this cycle route guide in 1947, many of the roads he mentions are now busier than they were and are not suitable for cycling today. Suggested alternative cycle routes, from Sustrans, which are in the same location as Harold's original route are listed below. To devise your own detailed route and map in the region, go to www.sustrans.org.uk for online mapping, free iphone and android apps.

The stunning Yorkshire Dales hosts a section of the National Cycle Network's most recent long-distance cycle route, the **'Way of the Roses'**. From **Settle** to **Pateley Bridge,** the route runs for 32 miles and takes in the most grueling climb with incredible views over the three Yorkshire peaks: Whernside (736m), Ingleborough (723m) and Pen-y-ghent (694m). The Way of the Roses is a coast-to-coast route from Morecambe to Bridlington and is quickly becoming one of the most popular cycle routes in the UK.

The Yorkshire Dales also has its very own 130-mile signed circular route, the **Yorkshire Dales Cycleway,** which is **Regional Route 10** of the National Cycle Network. The route features many challenging climbs and breathtaking descents on quiet lanes through the more remote parts of the Dales.

Useful maps and books (available from www.sustransshop.co.uk): *Way of the Roses Cycle Map; Yorkshire Dales Cycle Way; Yorkshire Dales for Cyclists; Off-road Trails & Quiet Lanes: Cycling in the Lake District & Yorkshire Dales.*

PART III

THE NORTH-EAST COAST

INTRODUCTION

THE part of Yorkshire that lies between the estuaries of the River Tees and the River Humber and is bounded on the east by the North Sea and on the west by the main L.N.E.R. line from London to Edinburgh contains within it a surprising variety of scenery. The hill country never attains the splendour reached by the Lake District or the character of the Pennine Dales, but in compensation the coast between Bridlington and Saltburn is finer than any other stretch of its length on the eastern side of the country.

Much of the inland area is dull, however, but the parts that are lacking in interest for the touring cyclist are well-defined and in any case are not spoilt by coal-mining or other heavy industries as much of South Yorkshire is. Holderness, the district south of the hilly chalk of the Yorkshire Wolds, is noteworthy only for its churches, the most outstanding of which is Beverley Minster. The chalk range itself, stretching from a little east of York, near Stamford Bridge, to the striking cliffs of **Flamborough Head**, is quiet country for the most part, not dramatic except at Flamborough, but exhibiting throughout a remarkable level of interest to the rider willing to explore.

On the east the district is bounded by the rich Plain of York, mostly based on the new red sandstone, with few scenic highspots, although full of small towns of coaching times and with the great wide flood of the River Ouse as a recurring feature. On the Ouse, of course, is **York**, without question one of the most fascinating towns in the whole of England and for many years a magnet for the cyclist, both record-breaker and tourist.

North of the chalk wolds, beyond the wide and shallow valley of the River Derwent, comes the finest region in north-east England for cycle-touring, the district of valley, fell and seashore called generically (and not altogether aptly) the Yorkshire Moors and Coast.

North-east Yorkshire, away from certain of the more popular

seaside resorts, is remarkably free from visitors. Of the bigger coastal resorts, Bridlington is busy and bustling; Filey quiet and ideal for the family man; Scarborough the largest and most varied; Whitby the most romantic in situation; and Saltburn and Redcar, for all their modernity, rather too far north for the best of the scenery. Any one of these, however, would serve the tourist who likes to have a town as a base and wishes to mix a conventional holiday with a few days' centre touring.

Scarborough Castle

The smaller coastal villages, notably' **Robin Hood's Bay**, Runswick Bay and Staithes, are (despite modern buildings in their hinterlands) intrinsically unspoilt. The gem is the charming little resort of Robin Hood's Bay, where a lane that has toppled off the main Scarborough-Whitby road decides to plunge straight into the sea betweeen the red roofs of the cottages that overlook the bay. Runswick, north of Whitby, is less compact but nearly as charming while uninhibited Staithes, more workaday than either of its two rivals, clusters around the mouth of a small valley.

Inland there are great spreading moorlands that are cut deep by long valleys which have no regular system as in the western dales. Bilsdale and Ryedale are perhaps the finest of these valleys, while the latter has within it the grandest of all the great Yorkshire abbeys, **Rievaulx** (see pages 79–80). West and east of Bilsdale is a district full of old tracks, some of them fairly smooth in surface. At one point, near Rosedale Abbey, the rideable route of an old mineral line provides some of the most satisfying aerial cycling in Britain, akin to the old miners' paths in the Lowther Hills, above Wanlockhead, in Scotland.

Although the great moorland mass is part of the Cleveland Hills, two outlying sections deserve separate attention. These are the Hambleton Hills, rising from the Plain of York to the east of Thirsk, and the Howardian Hills, a little to the south. About here are some of the most delightful villages and hamlets in England. **Coxwold** for instance, with its strange church and old houses, rivals Burford, in the Cotswolds, in character, while picturesque Hawnby and Lastingham are remoter haunts. Even on the main road from Pickering to Scarborough, the village of **Thornton-le-Dale** is most attractive, with a main street which has a stream for company.

Those cyclists who love the moorlands will find that the road between Pickering and Whitby is one of the most satisfying in the country. Goathland, just to the west of this highway (which is admittedly crowded enough on a summer's week-end) is a small, bright resort for those who seek the moors. It has three pleasing little fosses (or waterfalls) quite close and is in all ways an admirable centre for a combined cycling and walking holiday.

To the north lies the valley of the Yorkshire Esk, running from west to east and emptying itself into the North Sea at Whitby. The roads in the upper reaches of Eskdale have a way of keeping away from the valley, with the best bits about Glaisdale and Beggars' Bridge, the latter a graceful single-span built, according to legend, by a returned lover who was thwarted earlier from a final meeting with his girlfriend by the absence of a bridge.

Between the Esk Valley and the coast at Redcar and Saltburn the country is partly spoilt by the Cleveland iron-ore industry, yet in spite of this, the country south of the railway line westwards from Staithes is diverse and attractive.

The principal feature of the Cleveland Hills is the perky little peak of **Roseberry Topping**, between Guisborough and Stokesley. The hill is a decided landmark, although its summit is a mere 1,022 ft. above sea level. A little to the south is the Captain Cook Monument, a reminder that the famous sailor went to school at nearby Great Ayton and was apprenticed at Staithes.

The Cleveland and Hambleton Hills fall away on the west into the wide Vale of York. Here the cyclist who likes to plot long cross-country journeys from the map will be in his element. The greatest of the highways through the plain is the modern line of the Great North Road along the straight Roman road between Boroughbridge and Catterick Bridge. The sensible tourist will, however, give this highway a wide berth. There are many alternatives to the main roads through the Plain of York, an outstanding one being the lane route from York to Richmond via Brafferton, Topcliffe, Kirkby Wiske and Langton.

The four-day tour given in the next section might well be extended to seven or ten days with judicious use of the suggested bases. The writer confesses to a predilection for Robin Hood's Bay and the Coxwold area as centres; the one for the coast and the moors and the other for the valleys and foothills. In the more northerly part of the district, Castleton is perhaps the best choice.

Accommodation in the north-east part of Yorkshire is mostly of the homely type—farms and inns—and except at the more popular of the seaside resorts farmhouse fare is the staple, and prices are, on the whole, much more reasonable than in the Lake District and other touring districts of greater fame. The roads are now mostly in first-class condition, except on some of the more remote of the moorland crossings and on the culs-de-sac that drop down to the sea.

Camping sites may be found readily in the north-eastern part of Yorkshire. Some of the larger seaside camps will be too large and noisy for the average cycle tourist, who seeks quiet above all things. The writer has used good sites on the cliffs at Gristhorpe, north of Filey, and on a little piece of land above Robin Hood's Bay owned by Mr. Fewster, a local butcher. Inland there are plenty of farmers willing to accommodate cycle campers. Youth hostellers have a good deal of choice, with accommodation at Bridlington, Filey, Scarborough, Robin Hood's Bay, Rosedale, Castleton, Ampleforth, Malton and York.

APPROACHES

The City of York is without doubt the handiest of all starting places for a tour of the Yorkshire moors and coast. From everywhere south and south-west the city is a focal point for the district. Nevertheless, wheelmen from Hull and from Newcastle and Scotland can join the round tour presented later, the Hull riders at Scarborough and the northerners at Hasty Bank, approaching the latter point from Darlington by way of a lane route through Yarm.

Both York and Darlington are on the main L.N.E. line between King's Cross and Edinburgh. York is also well served by trains from the Eastern Counties (via March), and L.N.E. and L.M.S. services from Leeds, Bradford, Manchester, Liverpool and Birmingham; while there are other direct links with Sheffield, Derby, Leicester, Bristol and the South Coast.

Road approaches to York are excellent too, the Great North Road variant from London by way of Stevenage, Grantham, Retford, Doncaster and Selby being approximately 197 miles, fast, and for most of the way full of inns and other memories of the old coaching days. Riders from Nottingham and Derby could travel by Mansfield and Worksop, to Doncaster, through some of the newer colliery districts that do not suffer from bad roads as much as the older mining areas. Leeds and Bradford riders have direct access to York by Tadcaster, while from Manchester there is a hilly route across the Pennines by way of Oldham, Denshaw, Outlane, Cooper Bridge and Dewsbury, there taking the Leeds road to Tingley, where right and left soon to Rothwell, Woodlesford, Swillington, Garforth, Sherburn-in-Elmet, Cawood, Naburn and York. This provides a somewhat roundabout but relatively smooth route without entering any of the larger West Riding towns.

From Liverpool the best approach (although less direct than the industrialized and severely graded route by St. Helens, Bolton, Rochdale, Halifax and Leeds) is by Ormskirk, Preston, Whalley, Clitheroe, Gisburn, Skipton, Ukley, Otley and Wetherby. Bolton and Blackburn riders could join this line of approach at Whalley, while those from Burnley and Nelson could reach it at Skipton.

Birmingham and Midland riders will find it better to approach York by Derby rather than cross the Lancashire industrial belt, the Pennines and the West Riding textile district.

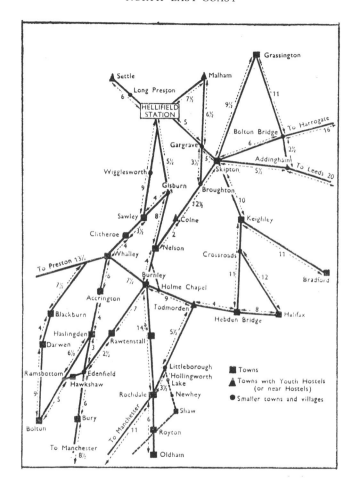

Approaches to York (Diagram not to scale)

A FOUR-DAY TOUR FROM YORK
OF 168 MILES

Leave York by Walmgate and Lawrence Street to Grimston Smithy (3 miles). Here turn left along a rural highway to Gate Helmsley and Stamford Bridge (8½), the site of a diversionary skirmish in 1066 before the Battle of Hastings. The river scenery hereabouts, on the Derwent, is good.

Continue along the road (on the line of a Roman artery) to the foot of **Garrowby Hill**, a rise of two miles from almost sea level to 808 ft., ending on the roof of the Yorkshire Wolds, the chalk hills that extend to the coast. There is a fine view westerly from the summit (15 miles from York). Over uplands to Fridaythorpe (19), an exposed village, immediately beyond which turn left and downhill into a dry, waterless dale reached at Fimber (21), and then go in a north-easterly direction, through more wooded country into **Sledmere** (25), home of the Sykes family that beautified this bare country with trees, buildings and agriculture.

Avoid the first turning on the left in Sledmere village and take the second (close to the inn) for **Rudston**, traversing lonely wold country and going easterly over all crossroads. At Rudston visit the church and examine, near its north-east corner, an ancient monolith, a single standing stone, 25 ft. of which are above ground. The church has a Norman tower.

Make then for **Bridlington** (41), passing through Boynton. Bridlington is a popular seaside resort, chiefly of value to the cycle tourist as a base from which to commence an exploration of the cliff scenery of Flamborough Head, five miles to the east at the northerly tip of Bridlington Bay, and Bempton Cliff, facing northwards.

The way to Flamborough village from Bridlington is obvious and, during the holiday season, much frequented. In about three miles the road crosses Dane's Dyke, a grass-grown embankment similar to the Devil's Ditch, west of Newmarket, in Cambridgeshire, and also built across chalk country. The purpose of both embankments was presumably defensive—Maginot lines of early historical times.

Flamborough village is not of any great interest. It is a large farming and fishing centre amidst the treeless plateau of Flamborough. The white tower of **Flamborough Head Lighthouse** becomes more prominent during the last mile or so to the road end close to the coastguard station (46). The lighthouse can be visited on foot. It is 82 ft. in height and situated a little way back from the edge of the cliffs. Visitors are admitted at intervals during the day. The views along the coast are first-rate.

From the coastguard station at Flamborough Head the cyclist can follow a footpath northwards to the picturesque cove called North Landing, following the edge of the cliffs. The chalk, here jutting boldly into the sea, looks its best on a bright summer's day, when the blue sea harmonizes with the white cliffs.

From North Landing the edge of the cliffs may be followed farther northwards at the expense of some lifting over fences and stiles. The quest here is for the steep, bold faces of the cliffs at **Bempton** and **Speeton.** Caution should be exercised, however, in wheeling the bicycle along the edge of the cliffs, as subsidences are fairly common. Prudence will advise where to keep well away from the lip of the fields.

Bempton and Speeton cliffs are over 300 ft. high, and the haunt of countless sea birds. During the month of May the cliffs become the scene of a spectacular egg-gathering show. Men (locally called 'climmers') are let down the cliff on ropes, and they collect the eggs from the ledges amidst a great uproar from the birds. The eggs are much sought after as delicacies by the Bridlington holidaymakers.

The view northwards from Speeton Cliff is very fine, with Filey Bay curving round in a grand arc to the jutting reef called Filey Brigg.

The cyclist should not continue to Speeton Cliff, but turn inland along a cart-track to Bempton village (53), a cosy haunt that has an inn where the stories of the 'dimmers' can be heard.

NOTE. In bad weather it is advisable to restrict a visit to Flamborough to the lighthouse and the North Landing, cutting inland from Flamborough village to Bempton, a saving of about two miles in distance.

There is some overnight accommodation at Bempton and **a** little more at Reighton, on the road to Filey, or at Hunmanby, off the road, to the left. There is, however, more likelihood of bed and breakfast (except during late July and August) at **Filey** (61), a bright but quiet resort, well situated close to the dark reef of Filey Brigg, which is a thrusting piece of hard rock from which the upper surface of the softer clays, seen in the crumbly cliffs south and north of Filey, has been washed away. There is a picturesque glen north of the promenade at Filey, and the trees around the town are welcome after the bareness of the Flamborough upland. There is a youth hostel at Filey. From Filey the 'coast' road north-westwards to Scarborough should be taken. Although spoilt in some sections by building, the natural beauties of the coastline, particularly at Cayton Bay, still manage to charm the eye. Those who cannot find accommodation at Filey might well try at Scarborough, where there is also a youth hostel.

Scarborough (67), by far the handsomest of all the Yorkshire coast resorts, and, with the exception of Whitby, the most strikingly situated, has pleasures to suit every taste, and is certainly well worth a morning's exploration. (See page 87.)

Ride round the headland from South Bay into North Bay by the marine drive, noting on the crags to the left the Norman keep, 200 ft. above the sea. Continue northwards by Scalby Mill, Burniston and Cloughton, turning right here for **Hayburn Wyke** (75), a delightful valley, laid out with paths, that runs down to the sea rather in the manner of the Manx glens.

Regain the road and bicycle and then continue over the moorlands to **Ravenscar**, a village that once had great development plans. The place is perched high above the sea, and it is necessary to retrace your route for a short way to a lane that goes northward and plunges steeply down Stoupe Brow to the Stoupe Beck, close to where it enters the sea. This is all unfrequented country, despite the proximity of Scarborough. A better surfaced lane is soon gained, and this leads through the village of Fylingthorpe into **Robin Hood's Bay** (84), which is suggested as a halting-place. Here there is a youth hostel and also camping facilities. Robin Hood's Bay is undoubtedly one of the most romantic seaside resorts in Britain. If no accommodation can be found there the tourist should try Whitby.

NOTE. In bad weather for mixed tandem crews and the less adventurous, the hillier but smoother alternative route between Cloughton and Robin Hood's Bay is by the Flask Inn and the Whitby Road, turning right for Robin Hood's Bay some six miles short of Whitby. This road is rather longer in mileage but possibly shorter in time. It gives some grand moorland riding, but the descent on Fylingthorpe should be treated with the utmost care.

'Bay Town,' the alternative name for the village of Robin Hood's Bay, has a main street second only to that of Clovelly in steepness. Many of the houses are built on the edge of the vertical cliffs. (See page 70.) For the family cyclist who is seeking a quiet resort for a centre, Robin Hood's Bay could hardly be bettered in the North of England.

Leave Robin Hood's Bay by the climbing road by Fylingdales and High Hawkser, whence it is mostly downhill to the narrow estuary of the Esk and **Whitby** (90). This romantically placed resort has two distinct portions, the old town, situated below the east cliff, whereon stands the parish church and the ruined abbey, approached from the town by 199 steps, and the new town situated on the West Cliff. The picturesque red tiles of the old town are a conspicuous feature.

From Whitby climb by Flowergate and then along Upgang Lane and the coast road to the compact village of Sandsend, delightfully situated at the mouth of two ravines. Then climb Lythe Bank (a sharp rise of a mile) into Lythe village (94). Still ascending, continue until a crossroads near Mickleby village, where turn right into Ellerby. At the fork turn right and down to Runswick Bay (99), a sprawl of picturesque roofs and walls in irregular tiers above the sea. There are good sands for bathing in a very fine bay. Return to Hinderwell, on the main coast road and at the prominent road end, turn sharply right into **Staithes** (103).

The village of Staithes, situated at the foot of a steep descent, rivals Robin Hood's Bay in its old-worldliness. More workaday than its rival, however, it has one greater charm, for here, across a tiny estuary, the cliff called Colburn Nab rises and lends an added distinction to the scene. Note on the quay a tarred inn, 'Cod and Lobster.'

From Staithes take the Loftus road to Easington (106), where turn left and over moorlands to the main Whitby-Guisborough road at Wapley House, situated high on the hills.

NOTE. A recommended alternative for rough-stuff specialists between Staithes and Wapley House is to take the Loftus road for a short distance from Dalehouse and there to go left, later climbing to a ridge between the Easington and Roxby Becks that gives some fine aerial views of the valleys followed by these streams. This route emerges on the Whitby-Guisborough road about a mile east of Wapley House, and is approximately the same distance as the first route suggested.

Turn towards Guisborough, but a mile east of Wapley House fork take a secondary road forking left. When this bends left again in about half a mile, go straight on along an unmetalled road that later crosses another lane at White Cross and drops steeply into Commondale (114), a hillside hamlet somewhat marred by a brickworks. The country remains bare and wild until the watershed is crossed, whereon both scenery and the road improve as the village of **Kildale** (118) is approached.

Maintain a south-westerly direction and at the first T-road turn left to Battersby (120) and into Ingleby Greenhow village (122), beyond which, at a T-road, the way is left towards Helmsley. The ensuing climb to 842 ft. at the head of Hasty Bank is steep, but thereafter there is a pleasing descent through Bilsdale, passing **Chop Gate** (127), where there is a friendly inn. The road, although much 'improved' threads a long valley of the type familiar to those who know the lower parts of the narrower Yorkshire Dales, in the Pennine system to the west.

Villages are few and the farms and forests dot the hillsides and brighten the floor of the dale. Beyond the farm of Laskill the highway begins a mile-long ascent that leads to attractive upland, leaving the valley and its rich wooded scenery to the right. Hereabouts Bilsdale becomes Ryedale, although the same stream continues in the valley bottom. About four miles beyond Laskill, on a descent through woodlands, the fork for **Rievaulx Abbey** turns off to the right. This 12th-century ruin of Cistercian foundation (the first in Yorkshire) vies in situation even with Tintern or Bolton in its picturesqueness. The remains include a roofless choir in good preservation, transepts, refectory and parts of domestic buildings. The site of the nave is nothing more than a series of shapeless mounds, the result of treating the Abbey as a quarry in bygone days.

From Rievaulx it is a downhill run of three miles to **Helmsley** (140), a handsome small town, with a market cross and modern church, as well as the picturesque remains of a castle. Helmsley and the neighbourhood are recommended for sleeping quarters. Besides Helmsley, the villages of Wass, Coxwold, Ampleforth (youth hostel), Hovingham and Slingsby, all to the south, provide quarters for the cyclist.

From Helmsley next day the tourist should ride south to near Sproxton, there forking right across Wass Moor to descend by Wass Bank (a fine ravine) to **Wass** (146) and **Byland Abbey**, the remains of which consist of a west front and south transept. This is the attractive foothill country of the Hambletons, worth much more time than the passing tourist can spend.

Coxwold, the next and larger village, is a neat place with a wide main street, including a bold and ornate church with an octagonal tower. At Shandy Hall, also in Coxwold, lived Laurence Sterne, the incumbent of Coxwold and writer of *Tristram Shandy* and *Sentimental Journey*.

From Coxwold, lanes lead southwards to **Easingwold** (154), an agricultural centre typical of the Plain of York, from which a better highway goes south-eastwards towards York, through **Skelton**, where there is a good example of an Early English church. **York** (168) is entered by way of Bootham Bar. It is recommended that any spare time that the tourist has before returning home should be spent in York. (See page 88.)

NOTE. Tourists with only three days to spare instead of four could cut out the Staithes-Commondale-Rievaulx round (although it is preferable to include this) and return from Robin Hood's Bay to York by the following sporting route: Whitby, then along the Guisborough road to Egton Low

Moor, where left to Egton; downhill to Beggar's Bridge over the Esk and up into Glaisdale. Along the side of Glaisdale Beck and later up to Glaisdale Ridge. On meeting the road from Lealholm Bridge at moortop, turn left by the lonely farm of High Hamer to Rosedale Abbey. Climb steep Rosedale Chimney Bank (formerly a formidable motorcycle test hill) and along a better road to Hutton-le-Hole, Keldholme, Kirkby Moorside, Welburn, West and East Ness, Slingsby, through the private park of Castle Howard, and so to Barton Hill, on the Malton-York road, which follow to York. This is a trip of 60 miles through most varied country, including sections of the most severe rough stuff in north-east England.

SOME DAY TOURS FROM THE SUGGESTED CENTRES

THE FORGE VALLEY
(Filey to Filey—30 miles)

The best inland scenery within easy reach of Filey is to be found in the **Forge Valley**. This is a favourite tripper excursion from Scarborough, but, nevertheless, is a pathway to wilder moorland scenery beyond Hackness.

From Filey the direction is north-westwards, leaving the main Scarborough coast road at Gristhorpe, and travelling through Ebberston, Cayton, Irton and East Ayton to West Ayton, where the Forge Valley will be seen opening to the north. The road passes through a narrow, wooded defile that in about two miles expands into a green amphitheatre through which goes the Sea Cut, a waterway made to carry the waters of the Upper Derwent into the North Sea close to Scarborough instead of past Malton and into the Ouse not far from Selby. From **Hackness** village the tourist can either travel north-westwards to the hamlet of **Langdale End**, in attractive river-and-hill scenery, or go a little northwards to the Norman and Early English church of Hackness and to Hackness Hall. From these the road back to Scarborough climbs to a height of 534 ft. on Suffield Moor, drops on **Scalby**, and enters the resort by way of Falsgrave. The run from Scarborough to Filey may be accomplished by the 'coast' road through Cayton. This round, including the extension to Langdale End, is less than 30 miles, but a full day might be spent on it.

A MOORLAND ROUND FROM FILEY
(Filey to Filey— 65 miles)

A longer day trip from Filey would be to follow, first, the road to East Ayton, and then go by the road that skirts the foothills of the Yorkshire Moors to Brompton and on to the very pretty village of **Thornton-le-Dale**. The ascent of the moors to the north can be started here (instead of going into Pickering), passing the hollow called the Hole of Horcum (a miniature Devil's Punch Bowl) and the ancient inn of **Saltergate**, where the peat fire is never allowed to go out.

Thereafter it is all wild, unfenced moorland, presenting some typical pictures of the district, until the steep drop into the Esk Valley at **Sleights**. Whitby may be entered via Sleights and left by the severe main road to Scarborough via High Hawkser and the Flask Inn, reaching lower country at Cloughton and continuing to Filey via Scarborough and Cayton. This is a round of about 65 miles.

CLIFF PATH TO WHITBY
(Robin Hood's Bay to Robin Hood's Bay—13 miles)

Short cycling excursions are the feature of Robin Hood's Bay. For the rough-stuff enthusiast, the cliff path to Whitby may be traced. This first runs close to the railway, giving a fine view of Robin Hood's Bay from the North, and then, some 300 ft. above the sea, undulates to near **Saltwick Bay**, whence the way to Whitby Abbey and the East Cliff is obvious. The distance to Whitby by this route is some seven miles, and while there is a considerable amount of cycling, a total time of about two hours should be allowed. There are many stiles, and in places the path runs inland to keep clear of treacherous sections of the cliff. The total distance from Robin Hood's Bay and back is about 13 miles.

TO FALLING FOSS

(Robin Hood's Bay to Robin Hood's Bay—11 miles)

Another short and severe excursion from Robin Hood's Bay is to **Falling Foss**. 'Baytown' is left by the Fylingthorpe lane that climbs to the Whitby-Scarborough road at Low Moor. This road should be followed southwards for about three-quarters of a mile, when a by-road to the right leads through plantations to a fork at Red Gate, the highest point on the secondary road. The way is left to Little Beck, whence Falling Foss, a waterfall more remarkable for its pleasant situation than for volume, will be found a mile to the south, reached by a footpath on the east side of the stream.

The outward route is the one to use when returning, making a total of about 11 miles for the double journey.

TWO OTHER EXCURSIONS FROM ROBIN HOOD'S BAY

Two other delightful day trips from Robin Hood's Bay are to **Beggar's Bridge** and to **Goathland**. For the former take the road to Whitby and then follow the Esk Valley by Ruswarp, Sleights, Grosmont and Egton Bridge, returning by the same route, a total distance of 32 miles return. For the latter, climb Sleights Moor (on the Pickering road from Sleights), turning right beyond the summit some 2½ miles beyond Sleights and dropping into Goathland, a bracing upland resort. This also is a trip of about 32 miles return.

SUTTON BANK AND KILBURN
(Helmsley to Helmsley—25 miles)

The best short cycling excursion from Helmsley is to go back along the Rievaulx road for two miles (see page 79), there forking left into Ryedale and climbing to the moorland through Scawton, a remote and picturesque village beyond which the unfenced country is gained, consisting of open heath and isolated plantations. Suddenly, however, the land falls away to the right, and there is a vast panorama across the Plain of York to the distant Pennines. The view is akin to, but wider than that from Fish Hill, above Broadway, in the Cotswolds.

The descent of **Sutton Bank**, with its hairpin bend, needs care. It was once a formidable hill-climbing test for the motorist. In a hollow to the right can be seen **Gormire Lake**, one of Yorkshire's few natural sheets of water. A curiosity of the lake is that it has no visible feeder or outlet. There are only about four natural lakes in Yorkshire.

About two miles from the summit check downhill speed and look out for a lane on-the left, less than a mile before the village of Sutton. Enter this and follow the foothills of the Hambledon range by **Low** and **High Kilburn** (noting the outline of **Kilburn White Horse** on the hill above), **Oldstead**, **Byland Abbey**, **Wass** and **Ampleforth** (youth hostel), and so back to **Helmsley**. This is a round of 25 miles through some most varied country.

KIRKDALE AND FARNDALE
(Helmsley to Helmsley—25 miles)

Going eastwards from Helmsley, the finest short journey is to **Kirkdale** and **Farndale**. The Pickering road is first followed from Helmsley but beyond Nawton, where the main road forks rightwards, the direction is straight ahead to **Kirkdale**. The attraction here is the Kirkdale Cave, some 80 yds. long. When it was first explored in 1821 the remains of tigers and hyenas were found. The cave is on the east side of the stream, and on the west is Kirkdale Church, which has a sundial dated 1060. Above the church a path follows the well-wooded beck for some way, and is worth exploring.

Beyond the cave the by-road reaches a crossroads, where a lane runs leftwards to the hilltop hamlet and crossroads of Padmoor. Here the way is straight ahead into Gillamoor village. The valley below is Farndale, earmarked by Hull for waterworks developments. The River Dove—stream of Farndale—is crossed at Lowna Farm, whence a side lane leads uphill to a turn, where right into the village which is misrepresented by the name of **Hutton-le-Hole**.

It is worth the while of the thorough tourist to continue eastwards from Hutton to the village of Lastingham, like most of these foothill settlements, romantic alike in situation and associations. The main feature of its village church is the crypt, an extensive one, reached by a flight of stairs from the middle of the nave above. To the west side of the graveyard there is a curious epitaph, relating to a blacksmith, and presumably written in advance by him. It runs:

> *My anvil and my hammer lie declin'd,*
> *My bellows, too, have lost their wind;*
> *My fire's extinct, my forge decay'd,*
> *And in the dust my vice is laid;*
> *My coals are spent, my iron's gone,*
> *My nails are driv'n, my work is done.*

After a climb southwards over moorland, the neat village of Appleton is entered, and after that it is all downhill to the Pickering-Kirkby Moorside-Helmsley road, where the way is right into Kirkby Moorside, an historic townlet on rising ground, with old houses and a castle.

The return westwards to Helmsley calls for no directions. This is a day of 25 miles in very interesting country.

CENTRES IN EAST AND NORTH YORKSHIRE

BEVERLEY (Hull, 8). This country town, the capital of the East Riding, now partly a suburb of Hull, has two fine churches, and has been called, with some exaggeration, 'the Rouen of England'. The Minster is at the north end of the town, and is noble and striking in its proportions. In beauty of detail and effect it is one of the finest churches in England. The total interior length is 334 ft., while the great transept has a width of 167 ft. The West Front, in the Perpendicular style, consists of a large west window to the nave. The Minster was founded in the eighth century by John of Beverley.

At the south end of Beverley, nearly a mile from the Minster, is St. Mary's Church, again mainly Perpendicular in style. Another feature of Beverley is the North Bar, the sole remaining gate of the town.

BRIDLINGTON (Scarborough, 16). A popular resort on a wide bay, properly called Bridlington Quay and three-quarters of a mile from the old town. The most historical building is the Priory, founded in the reign of Henry I. It has a good west front. Bridlington is the closest town to the scenery of Flamborough Head.

DRIFFIELD (Bridlington, 12). A market town and road centre at the southern end of the Yorkshire wolds, and a useful halt on the way to Bridlington. (Market day, Thursday.)

FILEY (Scarborough, 7). A neat, modern resort on Filey Bay, with fine sands stretching from the northern horn of the bay at Filey Brigg to Speeton Cliff. 'The Brigg' is a jutting reef, uncovered for an hour or two at low water, and suitable for picnicking or a lazy day. The north side is the steepest, and the south side is full of boulders. A cliff walk to Scarborough via Cayton Bay is one of the minor delights of Filey. The way is fairly obvious, and there is little to displease the eye until the main Filey-Scarborough road is joined about three miles south of the latter place.

HELMSLEY (Scarborough, 31; Pickering, 14; Thirsk, 13). One of the most attractive of the smaller Yorkshire towns, and a useful centre for Ryedale, Bilsdale and Rievaulx Abbey, as well as for the foothills of the Hambleton Hills and the Howardian Range. Much of the surrounding district is covered on pages 83–85, but a further delightful run is south-eastwards via Hovingham and Slingsby to Castle Howard Park, with a glimpse of (and occasionally an entry to) Castle Howard, a large, palatial mansion built by Vanbrugh in 1702. A little farther south (via Welburn) is Kirkham Abbey, well situated on the River Derwent, and with a gateway and manor house.

HULL. The commercial capital of East Yorkshire, and an important port and industrial centre (heavily attacked from the air during the war of 1939-45). Hull lies off the track of the average tourist, and is approached from the south by way of Thorne, Rawcliffe and a new bridge to Howden. The countryside is flat, but hereabouts the local cycling clubs are full of keen enthusiasts, who usually make for the hills north of the Thirsk-Scarborough road at week-ends. The plague of level crossings in the city is abating a little, and there are frequent steamers (carrying bicycles) across the estuary of the Humber to New Holland and the quiet and quaint touring district around the mouth of the River Trent, in Lincolnshire.

Hull's closest seaside resorts are Withernsea and Hornsea, on the North Sea, which is constantly encroaching on the soft coast. A run through Holderness, as the district between Hull and the sea is called, is full of architectural and agricultural interest. The route suggested is via Hedon (formerly a great seaport and with a fine church called the 'King of Holderness'), Patrington (with another fine church, the 'Queen of Holderness', the tower of which commands a fine view), and Kilnsea (subject to constant encroachment by the sea), whence it is possible to follow a raised causeway to Spurn Head, at the mouth of the River Humber. Then, turning northwards, by zig-zagging lanes, to Easington and Withernsea (a modern resort close to the site of engulfed villages), Aldbrough (a town of great antiquity) and Hornsea, the favourite resort of Hull people, with a shrinking mere to the landward and fine coast walks. The return route to Hull is via Seaton and. Skirlaugh or by a lane alternative a little to the south-east. This Holderness round totals about 68 miles, mostly in dead-flat country.

MALTON (York, 18; Scarborough, 22) . A main-road town of ancient foundation, Malton is a pleasant centre lying on the River Derwent, between the Yorkshire Moors and the Wolds. Old Malton church is the most impressive building in the immediate district. A few miles south west are the ruins of Kirkham Abbey, also on the Derwent.

PICKERING (Scarborough, 18; Whitby, 21). A handy centre for the Yorkshire Moors. The 14th century church contains some interesting monuments. The road northwards to Whitby runs across Pickering Moor, open and wind-swept. The railway takes an easier course and traverses valleys miles away from roads. There are about four trains every day in each direction.

SCARBOROUGH (York, 40). The largest and best-known of all the Yorkshire coast resorts. Quayside scenes to delight the photographer, a Norman castle on a peninsula 200 ft. above the sea, a fine Marine Drive, a concert place called 'The Spa', fine sands, clean streets, quiet valleys and many hotels and restaurants, all tend to make Scarborough one of the best 'centres' in Yorkshire for a cycling tour. Those who prefer quieter surroundings will find them at Filey, to the south, and at Robin Hood's Bay, to the north. But no visit to the Yorkshire coast would be complete without a visit to Scarborough.

SELBY (York, 14). An old town, now turned to manufacturing, situated well down the River Ouse, but on the direct road from Doncaster and the South to York. The much-restored abbey church was founded in the 11th century.

WHITBY (Pickering, 21; Scarborough, 20). An old fishing port at the mouth of the narrow estuary of the River Esk. The new part of the town is the West Cliff (the Esk enters the North Sea in a northerly direction), but the older and more picturesque section lies on the east side of the water, where old, red-tiled houses fill the narrow level between the tide and the cliffs. On the latter, gained by 199 steps, stand the sprawling parish church and the remains of Whitby Abbey, the latter exposed to all the winds that blow. The remains include the choir, with its north aisle, the north transept, parts of the west front and the windows of the north aisle. The church nearby stands on sloping ground closer to the estuary, and is made up of a variety of architectural styles, including a battlemented tower. Internally the furnishings are striking, and include a three-decker pulpit.

Amongst evening walks from Whitby, perhaps the best is along the coast to Sandsend; first for a mile along the low cliff north-westwards, and then on the sands. If permission can be obtained, the grounds of Mulgrave Castle, beyond Sandsend, are worthy of exploration. The return journey is some five miles, with this halved by the use of the train or 'bus from Sandsend.

In contrast to the coast, there is an excellent valley walk through the fields to Ruswarp, keeping close to the Esk at some points. This is about four miles in all.

YORK. The walled city of York, situated on the River Ouse, at the junction of the three Ridings, is one of the oldest cities in Britain. The capital of a Roman province, and with the considerable population of 10,000 at the time of the Doomsday Book, York has seen much history, and after the Saxons had retaken it from the Normans, William sacked the city and laid waste the entire area between the Humber and the Tees. In the Wars of the Roses the city was a centre of strife, and again in the Civil War, when it figured in the incidents that led to the defeat of Prince Rupert at nearby Marston Moor.

The outstanding building in York is, of course, York Minster, that towers over the city and beckons the cyclist to the city from whatever direction he approaches it. The Minster is normally open to visitors during the daytime. In dimensions it is second only to St. Paul's as the largest cathedral in Britain. Internally it is the most impressive of all great British churches. Architecturally it represents all the styles from Saxon to Perpendicular, the latter, with Decorated, being the principal element. The building is founded on the site of a wooden oratory erected in the year A.D. 627. Subsequent stone structures were all burnt down, but when the Normans had settled down, the foundation of much of the present edifice was laid.

The most striking external feature of York Minster is undoubtedly the West Front, which is in the Decorated style, and unequalled by any other of its kind in the country. Another strong point is the Central Tower, which rises to a height of 180 ft., and which may be ascended by the visitor by means of successive flights of steps. From the top there is a fine view of the Plain of York, extending from the Wolds (to the east) and the Moors (north) to the outlying flanks of the Pennines to the north-west. Closer at hand, the red and grey roofs of the town and the windings of the Ouse form a memorable picture. There is a handy official guide to York Minster on sale in the city.

Among other interesting 'sights' in York are St. Mary's Abbey and Museum, the latter containing a Roman pavement discovered in Micklegate. Although not as complete as those of Chester (which form a continuous promenade), the city walls of York form a circuit of nearly three miles. It is not, however, either convenient or desirable to make the full circuit. The finest parts are at the Bars, or entrances to the mediaeval city. Bootham Bar, north-west of the Minster, is a good starting-off point, and consists of a plain, round double arch on an Edwardian base. From here the wall may be followed north-eastwards, and then south-eastwards to Monk Bar (across the Scarborough road), the loftiest of all the gates, with a portcullis chamber and battlemented gallery. Next on in this clockwise perambulation comes the site of Layerthorpe Postern, followed by the Red Tower (brick) and Walmgate (across the Bridlington highway), which retains its barbican. Close to Fishergate Postern is the churchyard of St. George's, in which Dick Turpin was buried (1739). Beyond Skeldergate Bridge the wall is regained at Skeldergate Postern and the artificial mound called Baile Hill, reaching a height of 40 ft. and hidden in trees. Finally comes Micklegate Bar, at the south-west corner, guarding the outlet to Leeds and the Great North Road, the most important gate of all. A plain, round arch is surmounted by a massive stone tower, and on the battlements are figures of men-at-arms. Between Micklegate Bar and Bootham Bar the interest decreases, except for the view of York Station, built handsomely on a curve, and one of the largest and busiest in Britain.

There are several old churches in the city and also a castle, the latter occupying a site of four acres and surrounded by a wall 35 ft. in height. The castle includes modern buildings and the Edwardian Clifford's Tower, named after the custodians, a notable Yorkshire family. Closer to the Minster are to be found the narrow streets that formed part of the mediaeval city. Some of these suffered in the 'Baedeker raids' of the Luftwaffe during the 1939-45 war. The most famous of the streets is 'The Shambles', so called from its being the former headquarters of the city's butchering trade. There is a noteworthy peep at the Minster tower from The Shambles.

It remains to be said that York is famed also for its river boating, for the frequent visits for their Easter annual meet by members of the National Clarion C.C., for its chocolate and cocoa factories, its associations with the Society of Friends, its youth hostel and its situation at the end of one of the most famous cycling pilgrimages, from London to York via the Great North Road.

The Shambles, York

PLATE I

Photo J.D. Heald

FRIAR'S CRAG, DERWENTWATER

photo. L. Dover

HONISTER CRAG FROM CRUMMOCK WATER

photo. L. Dover

ENNERDALE WATER

photo. L. Dover

WASTWATER AND GREAT GABLE

Photo. "Cycling"

LANGSTRATH, BETWEEN THE STAKE PASS AND BORROWDALE

Photo. W. Swindon

WRYNOSE BOTTOM, SEEN FROM HARDKNOTT PASS

Photo. "Cycling"

GORDALE SCAR

PLATE VIII

Photo. "Cycling"

MALHAM COVE

Photo. "Cycling"

SWALE BRIDGE, NEAR RICHMOND

Photo. C. H. Wood

KILNSEY CRAG

STAITHES VILLAGE

Photo. V. Hey

COLLECTING GULL'S EGGS, BEMPTON CLIFF

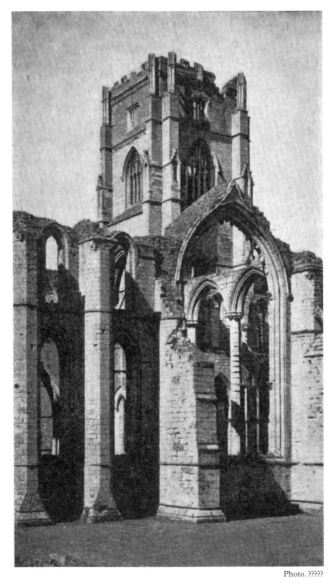

FOUNTAINS ABBEY

Photo. F. Smith

THE ROMAN ROAD, BLACKSTONE EDGE

KNARESBOROUGH

Photo. C. H. Wood

RICHMOND, YORKSHIRE

Cycling along the
North-East Coast today

As Harold Briercliffe wrote this cycle route guide in 1947, many of the roads he mentions are now busier than they were and are not suitable for cycling today. Suggested alternative cycle routes, from Sustrans, which are in the same location as Harold's original route are listed below. To devise your own detailed route and map in the region, go to www.sustrans.org.uk for online mapping, free iphone and android apps.

The Yorkshire Coast is attracting more cyclists than ever since the opening of the 169-mile **Way of the Roses** cycle route, which finishes in Bridlington. Using the route to descend into **Bridlington**, you are treated to fantastic views of Flamborough Head and a taste of the beauty of the landscape further up the coast.

National Cycle Network Route 1 runs for 47 miles from **Bridlington** up to **Whitby** along the Yorkshire coast, where there is a small break in the route before it picks up again at **Staithes**. A wonderful 20-mile winding converted railway path runs from **Scarborough** up to **Whitby** via the picturesque Robin Hood's Bay. Whitby is also the start or finish of the **Walney** to **Whitby coast-to-coast cycle route.**

Useful maps and books (available from www.sustransshop.co.uk): *Yorkshire Wolds, York & Hull (Sustrans Cycle Route Map); Way of the Roses (Sustrans Cycle Route Map).*

PART, IV

SHORTER TOURS AND CONNECTING ROUTES

THE RIBBLE VALLEY AND FOREST OF BOWLAND

(Preston to Lancaster—60 miles)

To the east of the London-Carlisle main road (A6), where it strides across the flats between Preston and Lancaster, lies the varied country of dale and open fells called the Ribble Valley and the Forest of Bowland.

> **NOTE**. Ribblesdale is the country around the upper parts of the course of the Ribble, down as far as Gisburn. Below that comes the Ribble Valley.

A detailed exploration of the area is possible for the tourist who is heading for the Lake District or the Yorkshire Dales. Indeed, a visit might be prescribed as an essential prelude to these regions of greater fame. The Ribble and Bowland country will not lose greatly in the comparison.

The experienced North- and Mid-Lancashire day rider and weekender regards this district as his own particular province. The diversity of scenery is remarkable and, once off the main roads there is plenty of quiet. For the cycle camper the area has much to commend it, as most of the land is given over to dairy farming rather than arable, and streams and woods are plentiful. In the heart of Bowland, which lies between the river country of **Mitton** and **Sawley** to the south and the lonely, sweeping fells to the north, is **Slaidburn,** where there is a long-established youth hostel that would serve admirably as headquarters for a three-day exploration. Bed-and-breakfast accommodation is not easy to find, but Slaidburn, nearby Newton, Dunsop Bridge, Waddington, Chipping and Longridge (the latter closer to Preston) are worth trying.

The district is pre-eminently a cycling one, as the distances are too great for walkers, and the motorcar cannot penetrate far into the twisting and hilly lanes. The latter piece of optimism does not apply to the main routes through the district at week-ends, and the wise cyclist will keep away from the popular 'Trough of Bowland' road from **Whitewell** and **Dunsop Bridge** to Marshaw, Quernmore and Lancaster, on Sundays. On the other hand, there are lane routes in Bowland that are undisturbed even when the holidaymakers of Preston, Blackburn, and the smaller Lancashire weaving towns turn out in their thousands.

Those cyclists with a hankering after antiquities will find that at **Ribchester** there is the site of one of the most important Roman stations in the country. Ribchester is approached from the Preston-Whalley main road at Oaks Bar, close to which there are several catering places, notably the Ribble Valley Clarion Clubhouse, open to all cyclists, and with catering and overnight accommodation facilities as well as tennis courts and a football field. A steep descent leads to the handsome, if narrow, Ribchester Bridge, and thereafter to Ribchester's Roman remains. Note in passing the ancient and picturesque almshouses and tiny church of Stydd and the quite remarkable white bull, which serves as a sign at the hostelry of that name.

North of Ribchester the land climbs to the long whalebacked hill called Longridge Fell. Above the manufacturing town of **Longridge** stands the western summit of the fell, called Tootal Height, from which there is a notable panorama, extending westward across the flat, fertile Fylde (or 'field') to the pleasure city of Blackpool and its tower. On the south side of the fell stand the extensive grounds and stately buildings of **Stonyhurst College**. The grounds may be entered by the passing cyclist, while those armed with a letter of introduction from a Roman Catholic priest may enter the premises. A prior notice to the Rector is advisable, however. At Stonyhurst there is a well-equipped astronomical observatory with a world-wide reputation. One of the most exciting events in recent times in this part of the world was the eclipse of the sun in May, 1927. Thousands of people (the writer included) went to this area in the early morning to witness the eclipse. Kemple End, the north-easterly corner of

Longridge Fell, was a favourite vantage point, but weather conditions were hardly helpful.

South of Stonyhurst the waters of the Rivers Ribble, Hodder and the Lancashire Calder meet. Of the three, the Hodder is the most picturesque, and at the **Lower** and **Higher Hodder** bridges the scenery is charming. At Lower Hodder there are two bridges, the oldest one (dated 1512) being narrow and covered with ivy. Over this bridge passed Cromwell in 1648, when on his way to the Battle of Preston, in which he defeated the Royalists. Not far away is **Mitton Church,** standing on a hillside. A leper window and many internal and external ornaments are amongst its features, with its leading highlights the Sherburne Chapel and monuments.

Two miles south of Mitton is the important road junction of Whalley, popular as a cyclists' meeting-place. Here, too, there is an old church, and also Whalley Abbey, which remains as a ruin with two gateways as the principal reminders of its former strength and importance. Whalley stands besides the sullied Lancashire Calder in a valley that is naturally beautiful, beneath the wooded hill called Whalley Nab and close to another good viewpoint named Clark Hill.

North-east of Mitton by a lane route that runs close to the Kibble at one point, is Waddington (like Mitton, also on the north bank, in Yorkshire), where a clear stream runs through the centre of the main street. Here is **Waddington Hall**, where Henry VI, in hiding, was betrayed into the hands of his enemies. South of the Ribble stands **Clitheroe**, the only large town in the Ribble Valley, except for Preston.

Still using the lanes on the north side of the Ribble, the cyclist can obtain splendid views of the great whaleback of Pendle Hill to the south (see page 114 for detailed particulars). Beyond Grindleton the road descends to the side of the Ribble at a delightful reach.

NOTE. It is worthwhile at this point to cross Sawley Bridge and also examine the scanty remains of Sawley Abbey and the two modern gateways that span part of the road.

Still farther on is the quaint village of **Bolton-by-Bowland**. Here the cross on the village green was famous in pre-war days as the rostrum for cycling rallies that drew C.T.C. members and others from all parts of Lancashire and Yor shire. The main features of the church are the Pudsay memorials, including a monument to the three wives and 25 children of one of this family.

From Bolton-by-Bowland a hill road runs north-westwards to **Slaidburn**, a large village amidst uplands and on the edge of lonely fells that stretch northwards to the Lune Valley. Slaidburn has a church dating back to the 12th century, and until recent years the curfew was rung.

Slaidburn is a convenient starting place for three good pass-storming routes. The first, called Bowland Knotts is to the north-east, and is reached by turning left at a crossroads some three miles along the Tosside road. It runs near the reservoir of the Fylde Water Board at Stocks-in-Bowland, and climbs across the upland, descending at length to Clapham, on the Settle-Ingleton road. The surface of this road has been improved in recent years, but it should be treated with caution.

Market Cross and Stocks, Bolton-by-Bowland

The second route, across **Tatham Fells**, is longer and more adventurous. It is gained by going northwards from Slaidburn to the farm of Kenibus and the headwaters of the River Hodder. Open fell and a rough track lead to a gated lane that drops into High Bentham, on the Clapham-Wennington road. This crossing is noteworthy for the views that it gives on a clear day of the fells of the West Riding, notably of Whernside, Ingleborough and Pen-y-Ghent.

The third crossing, by **Salter Fell**, is more of a true pass-storming route, lonely and grass-grown. The Kenibus road must be followed for a little over a mile from Slaidburn, when a rough road going left should be followed. At a T-point, the way is right, and so above Croasdale House to the source of the Croasdale Beck. Onwards, in a north-westerly direction, the way is along a grass-grown track keeping to the ridge. A long descent, with the River Roeburn flowing through a deepening valley on the left, leads to High Salter Farm and steeply into Roeburndale, whence the crossroads of Butt Yeats, on the High Bentham to Lancaster road, is reached after a straight, smooth slope. The two latter routes are for summer and clear days only. About two hours are needed from Slaidburn to Clapham by Bowland Knotts; about three from Slaidburn to High Bentham via Tatham Fells; and at least four hours from Slaidburn to Butt Yeats by Salter Fell.

South-west of Slaidburn is the grey hamlet of **Newton**, where John Bright, the 19th century statesman, spent two years of his youth and went to school.

Along an undulating road towards the west, still down the graceful valley of the Hodder, is **Dunsop Bridge**, a mere hamlet at the mouth of the **Trough of Bowland**. This is a wild upland hollow, threaded by a good road, that has achieved a wide fame. It is to be avoided on summer Sundays but it affords a striking run that has all the charm of variety. Beyond the hamlet of Sykes the road climbs fairly steeply, and then descends into a wooded hollow where it shares the valley-bottom with a brown trout stream.

At Marshaw, the first hamlet on the north side of the pass, a road breaks away to the left and leads through two watersplashes and over open moorland to Scorton village and the Preston-Lancaster road at Garstang.

Continuing towards Lancaster, the country is less romantic for a while. Just beyond the stone bridge at Lee, a right turn goes up to the remote hamlet of **Tarnbrook**, an ideal camping spot, with a farm and a cottage or two as the only reminder of the outer world.

High on Abbeystead Fell is a watch tower, from which there is a widespread view, extending north-westwards to the Lakeland mountains, westwards across the Fylde to Blackpool and its tower and southwards across the sweeping Wyresdale Fells.

A steep drop and rise by Quernmore lead into **Lancaster**, the county town, which has an old castle with a square keep, and oilcloth manufacture. Four miles west is **Morecambe**, popular with West Riding people as a resort, which, with the ancient village of **Heysham** (a port for Ireland nowadays), forms a useful 'centre' for cyclists wishing to base themselves on a seaside place. It is much closer to Lunedale and the Lake District than the larger Blackpool. From Lancaster, Kendal can be reached in 21 miles and Preston in 21½. The round described above can be linked up to form a thorough exploration of Bowland and Wyresdale of some 60 miles from Preston to Lancaster.

ROUND PENDLE HILL
(Whalley to Whalley—25 miles)

The road junction of Whalley, 26½ miles north of Manchester, and 14 miles north-east of Preston, makes a handy starting-point for a round of **Pendle Hill**, the most distinctive ridge in Lancashire south of the Lake District, and the summit that dominates most of the Ribble Valley. A visit can be worked in *en route* for Bowland Forest or the Yorkshire Dales, although then it would be convenient only to bring in the northern slopes between Whalley and **Gisburn**, the by-lane route on this side of the hill providing a slower but equally attractive route, as an alternative to the Ribble Valley trip described in the previous tour.

Accommodation in the Pendle Hill area is quite adequate, although it inclines towards providing for the needs of day trippers. Hereabouts there is a large trade in pots of tea (or 'tea only'), and even in sales of hot water ('bring your own tea and sugar'), but those with more pretentious desires can have them fulfilled. There are guest houses and farm houses that have spare beds at **Worston**, **Downham**, **Barley** and **Rough Lee**, as well as at Whalley, while on the southern side of Pendle, near Barley, there is a good farmhouse youth hostel. Camping sites, too, are plentiful.

About 1½ miles south of Clitheroe on the Whalley-Clitheroe road a by-lane strikes rightwards to Worston, a quaint hamlet that wears a prosperous look, and here a tree-shaded lane turns right and goes in 1½ miles to **Downham**, where grey tiers of farms and cottages form perhaps the prettiest village in this part of Lancashire. There is no hint of industrialism about it, and from the higher ground to the north the eye can range over a wide panorama that stretches across the wide and well-wooded valley traversed by the Ribble to the mountain giants of Ingleborough and Pen-y-Ghent.

Downham has a church of ancient foundation that provides a prominent landmark, but the main attraction is the domestic arrangement of the village, seen at its best from the road fork below the church and looking southwards across field and forest at the bold, dun form of Pendle Hill.

NOTE. From Downham the rider wishing to pick up the Bowland Forest route described in the previous chapter should travel through Rimington (the village that gave its name to the hymn tune) to Gisburn, another important road junction. From Gisburn, Hellifield (for the Yorkshire Dales) is 5½ miles, Nelson (for Burnley and Manchester) 6, and Skipton (for Leeds and Bradford) 11. From Gisburn a quiet lane leads by a bridge across the Ribble at an excellent 'bit' called The Kennels to Bowland-by-Bowland and the road for Slaidburn and Bowland Forest.

From Downham a lane climbs towards the south-east, gradually rising along the slopes of Pendle Hill and dipping now and again into doughs (or small wooded valleys) before rising sharply to the cross-roads at Annal Cross (an old boundary mark). Here the way is right to the summit of the pass at 1,137 ft. To the right is the the northern shoulder of Pendle, leading to the hill's highest level of 1,831 ft.

NOTE. From this point Pendle can be ascended readily and with no great difficulty, provided clear weather conditions prevail. The way up is obvious, although there is no regular path. The view from the summit of Pendle Hill is most extensive, ranging northwards across the richness of the Ribble Valley to the desolation of the striding ridges to the north. The flat-topped hill is Ingleborough, above Ingleton, the domed summit to the right (or east) being Pen-y-Ghent. Another ascent of Pendle—the one used most often—runs from Barley northwards along a fairly obvious slanting gully to the summit. This route is longer but easier than the direct assault mentioned above. The writer has a vivid recollection of being one of a party of campers that, on a November evening in the early 1930s, left Barley for the hilltop. We pitched on the very summit in a hollow and slept when the gale would let us. Next morning there was snow everywhere, and the northward view was a vision in white.

The south-east side of Pendle, called Pendle Forest, is wilder than the Ribble Valley front. The proximity of the north-east Lancashire cotton-weaving towns, too, is felt, although their influence on this nearby moorland country is smaller than might be expected. From Annal Cross there is a steepening drop into Barley village, on Pendle Water, the most important stream in these parts.

From Barley a road runs down Pendle Water, first by a mill and then through a wooded avenue, into the hamlet of Rough Lee. (The final piece of this road is not shown by Bartholomew. Nevertheless, the principal road into Rough Lee from the west runs alongside Pendle Water and into the hamlet, which has a picturesque situation.) The main part of Rough Lee climbs steeply uphill across a stone bridge.

Rough Lee was regarded between 1580 and 1612 as the G.H.Q. of the Lancashire Witches, immortalized by Harrison Ainsworth, the novelist. Two old women, Mothers Dem-dike and Chattox, were regarded as leaders of the band. They were without doubt wicked but almost certainly mad.

They were taken to Lancaster in 1612 and tried and sentenced to death for 'having bewitched to death by devilish practices and hellish means' 16 people of the district. Malkin Tower, no longer in existence, was the meeting place of the band, while Alice Nutter (with a surname still common in Lancashire) another of the accused, was a wealthy woman who lived at Rough Lee Hall, and was thought to have been a victim of a financial 'frame-up'. The Hall remains, although fast falling into decay.

From Rough Lee, after a little retracing, a short stretch of narrow lane leads into the hillside hamlet of **Newchurch**, whence a further by-lane goes westwards from above the church by pastoral scenes past the farms of Saddlers, Old Hall and Higher Town, to a ridge road running by Hill Top, and then into the valley of the Sabden Brook at the large manufacturing village of **Sabden**. Like many of the smaller and older cotton and woollen manufacturing centres, Sabden, with its stone houses, looks both prosperous and attractive. Richard Cobden, the 19th century statesman, was interested in Sabden, and did much early welfare work in the place.

NOTE. North-westwards from Sabden another side road climbs alongside a long row of cottages to the 'Nick O' Pendle'—exactly what the name implies—whence there is a swift fall into the Ribble Valley at Clitheroe. This route, with the Annal Cross road to the north east, completes a round that approaches Pendle Hill very closely. From Sabden a rural lane leads back into **Whalley**, the starting point.

This round of approximately 25 miles can be made to fit into a week-end from Manchester or Liverpool, or from Bradford or Leeds. From nearer towns the circuit is ideal for a day run. The whole atmosphere is one of homeliness and peace that is nearly always to be found in a district that is given over largely to sheep and dairy farming on the edge of moorlands. The Pendle district is perhaps at its best on a short winter's day, when motor traffic is absent and the landscape is bathed in golden sunshine.

THE BRONTE COUNTRY
(Hebden Bridge to Hebden Bridge—30 miles)

Haworth, the home of the Brontes, is only some nine miles west of Bradford, and lies on the edge of a wide moorland district that has not been over-run by any main roads or railways. The town is now a busy manufacturing centre, but the steep main street, the old Black Bull, the church and parsonage are sufficient in themselves to merit attention from the tourist who is making for the Yorkshire Dales or the Lake District and finds himself in Keighley, in the Aire Valley, four hilly miles to the north-east. The moorlands and their occasional deep ravines (as at **Hardcastle Crags**) are, however, a greater attraction than even the associations with the Brontes.

Once again, this is country more for the day-rider than the holidaymaker. There is overnight accommodation, however, at **Haworth**, **Stanbury**, **Hurstwood** and elsewhere, as well as camping facilities. There is a good youth hostel at **Jerusalem Farm**, north-east of Laneshaw Bridge and just off the route recommended, and also at **Mankinholes** (south-east of **Todmorden**, which is four miles short of **Hebden Bridge**, coming from Manchester), and at **Wainstalls** (north-west of Halifax, in another of the long, densely wooded valleys called Luddenden Dene). Either of the latter would serve as a base for the suggested route through the district: Mankinholes for those from the Lancashire side, and Wainstalls for visitors from the Yorkshire direction.

A round that gives a thorough insight into the district might start at Hebden Bridge, which is some 24 miles north of Manchester by road and rail, and also readily approached from Burnley and the North Lancashire cotton towns, as well as from Bradford and Leeds to the east, although over hilly roads.

Hebden Bridge should be left by the Keighley road, which immediately commences to climb out of the Calder Valley, and from a ledge commands a splendid prospect into the deep wooded vale called Hardcastle Crags (see page 121). The first village of **Pecket Well** marks the end of the intakes (or fields taken in from the moorland), and thereafter the moorland is mostly uncultivated. Less than a mile beyond Pecket Well, at an altitude of 1,067 ft., a lane strikes leftwards and runs in an up-and-down fashion over unmetalled gritstone, past the farm of Bedlam, to a sharp rise up a gully that leads over Sun Hill, and down by the side of Leeshaw Reservoir to the hamlet of Marsh; and so, up the 'setts' (or cobbles) of the steep main street of **Haworth**, to where the swinging sign of the Black Bull beckons.

The writings of three sisters, daughters of an incumbent of Irish extraction with a French name, together with the human weaknesses of their brother, have brought to this hilly Yorkshire townlet a fame that has spread—with the usual results—to the far corners of Hollywood. The setting of the inn, graveyard, church and parsonage is not as gloomy as portrayed by some earlier writers. Indeed, the droll enters into the impression as soon as the window is shown through which brother Branwell left the inn and escaped across the churchyard. The churchyard is full now and the parsonage is a museum, while the church is remarkable only for the vault beneath, in which lie all the Bronte family except Ann, who was buried at Scarborough.

A long mile to the west stands the old ridge village of **Stanbury** that marks the return to the wild upland again, and is perhaps more in keeping with the wild spirit of *Wuthering Heights* than modern Haworth. Close by, yet hardly worth a visit because of itself alone, is the so-called Bronte waterfall, on the Sladen Beck, where the introspective Emily turned for consolation.

Farther on is Ponden Reservoir, and on the opposite bank from the road stands Ponden Hall, identified with some of the scenes pictured by the sisters. The road now goes steadily upwards past a shooting lodge (these are grouse moors), and over into Lancashire. Just beyond the true summit a gateway to the left gives access to a rough upland cartway that eventually descends through a series of water-splashes to the remote corner of the county that comprises the hamlet of **Wycoller**.

A clear stream flows down the dell to enter the village close to a 13th century pack-horse bridge of double arches. There is another bridge, too, consisting of three large slabs on boulders, akin to the clapper bridge at Tarr Steps, in Somerset; while not far away a single-slab bridge recalls the bridges of Dartmoor. On the north side of the hamlet, to the right on entering from Haworth, stands ruined Wycoller Hall, the one-time home of two famous local families, the Hartleys and the Cunliffes. The unique feature of the building is the great fireplace. Wycoller Hall is reputed to be the original of Ferndean Manor in *Jane Eyre*, the rambling building to which Rochester retired when maimed and blinded, there to be comforted, in the long last, by Jane.

It is a short run from Wycoller to the industrial townlet of **Trawden**, and then, out of this, up to the moors again, to a hilltop cross-roads. Here the way is left, to the short, steep fall of Thursden Bank and the few trees of Thursden Brook, where this leaves the sterile upland for the friendlier farming lands. Following a mile of climbing, mostly along a narrow ledge overhanging a deep hollow, the moorland summit (1,217 ft.) is reached above Widdop Cross, another boundary mark, this one indicating the Lancashire-Yorkshire border. The cross will be found to the left, close to a bridge across a tiny stream, a short way down the descent.

The subsequent falling road past Widdop Reservoir is noteworthy for the plentiful evidence that the whole of this upland saucer was the scene of a glacial drift which scooped out the valley and left on the tops of its upraised flanks the normal debris of such action—boulders and 'edges' of gritstone—as well as at least one good rocking stone, so poised on a thin ridge that it can be swung from side to side.

A deep trough of woodland marks the end of the moorland once again, and the coming of the upper part of **Hardcastle Crags**, here called Blake Dean. On the descent, before a sharp hairpin, there is a small chapel on the left, famous as the haunt of the 'Henpecked Husbands,' a Yorkshire society, members of which come here once a year to escape the attentions of their wives.

Thereafter, as the valley of the Hebden Water deepens on the left and becomes Hardcastle Crags, the road hangs above it in an aerial fashion, giving revealing glimpses of the dark woods that fill the vale far below. The first village is Slack, like Stanbury, perched on a narrow neck of land and full of old houses. At the east end of the village the road forks, the left-hand one swinging away and clinging spectacularly above the Hebden Water, down into Hebden

Bridge (caution), the starting point. The whole round is barely 30 miles, but cannot be hurried owing to the hills and indifferent surfaces.

HARDCASTLE CRAGS

There are several other side excursions in this district that deserve visits, perhaps at separate times. Hardcastle Crags, for instance, is well worth exploration afoot. The valley is reached by a side road to the left off the Pecket Well road, rather more than half a mile out of Hebden Bridge. The bicycles can be left at the collection of old mills, houses and cottages near the main entrance to the valley. The path along the southern side of the valley is preferable to the drive on the north. The walker should travel at least as far as the stepping stones near the rocky mounds amidst the trees that give the valley its name. The river scenery is of a very high order, the brown, pebbly brook and the abundant trees making a delightful picture at any time of the year. Week-ends in summer, however, should not be spent at Hardcastle Crags, as the valley is something of a trippers' haunt.

'WUTHERING HEIGHTS'

From Stanbury a walk of about two miles leads first along a cart-road and then by a footpath (leading south-west of the village) climbs to Top Withens, the decaying upland farmhouse that is said to be the original of 'Wuthering Heights'. The surroundings are wild enough, the bold sweeping skylines, the rough moor-grass and the broken walls all fitting into the desolation. The farm, however, is much smaller than the commodious building that arose in the mind of Emily and in the cinema re-creation of the scene.

The visitor from Stanbury need not take his bicycle to 'Wuthering Heights'. Nevertheless, those who wish for a through route and do not mind pushing their bicycles along a moorland track can continue from Top Withens and inside a few minutes cross the ridge to the south and then strike along a footpath in a south-easterly direction to the chain of reservoirs at Walshaw Dean. From the reservoirs a rideable path, and then a typical gritstone road run down to **Blake Dean**, previously described, whence Hebden Bridge may be reached by way of **Slack**.

The footpath section of this route, from Stanbury to Walshaw Dean, is only a little over five miles long, needing about two hours, including time for sight-seeing, but should not be attempted in winter or in bad weather.

HURSTWOOD AND TOWNELEY HALLS

Closer to Burnley and gained by lanes to the right (or north) of the Todmorden-Burnley main road, are the ancient halls of **Hurstwood** and **Towneley**. Hurstwood is the more remote of the two, set in a little hamlet that lies up a cul-de-sac. The hall is a low stone house, with gables and steps down to the porch. The village is, incidentally, a noted cyclists' catering venue.

Also at Hurstwood is the 16th century house that was the home of Edmund Spenser, the great Elizabethan poet. Present-day northerners would have no difficulty in understanding him, for all his men were lads and his women lassies.

The turreted mansion of Towneley Hall now stands within a public park, and is the Burnley municipal museum. The sparrowhawk, the crest of the Towneleys, can be seen on the walls and rainpipes. A clock over the middle porch is 300 years old, and there is a secret hiding place, a relic of the days of the Reformation. There is a private chapel, too, and several rooms furnished in the fashion of earlier days.

CLIVIGER GORGE AND THE LONG CAUSEWAY

The Burnley-Todmorden-Hebden Bridge main road runs, some five miles from the former place, through the **Cliviger Gorge**. The cliffs to the south-west, as seen from the summit railway bridge, are bold and high, reaching up to the moorlands behind.

An alternative route, also connecting Burnley with Hebden Bridge, goes north of the valley road, and from **Mere Clough**, a hamlet south of Hurstwood, traverses the Long Causeway, a road of mediaeval (and possibly Roman) origin. It was used by the pack-horses of the days before the Industrial Revolution, when there was more life and activity in these uplands. The farming community of those times spent part of its time in woollen spinning and weaving, the finished product being carried to the markets on the backs of pack-horses. The long, low windows of the stone dwellings of the upland are evidence of this cottage industry, for as much light as possible was needed for the work.

At the eastern end of the Long Causeway is the straggling hamlet of **Blackshaw Head**, and below that, in a steep-sided valley, is the smaller settlement of **New Delight** (striking name!), where the writer remembers a snug inn.

From New Delight a lane runs down a vale to Mytholm, just west of Hebden Bridge. This route, despite the council houses towards its foot, is a most romantic one through the Colden Valley, reminiscent in its dense woodlands and steep sides of the Black Forest. The blackened gritstone crags strike a sombre note in winter.

High above the Colden Valley stands the church watchtower of Heptonstall, a sturdy hilltop village, best reached from New Delight via Slack village. The site must have commended itself early to the dwellers in these parts, for in prehistoric times it was high above the swamps and fogs of the uncleared Calder Valley. On a projecting hill between two side valleys, it was a position of great defensive strength. As late as the Civil War it figured in some stirring history.

THE LANCASHIRE COAST
(Liverpool to Cartmel—89½ miles)

The cyclist wishing to link up a North Wales tour with one in the Lake District or the Yorkshire Dales is faced with a crossing of the Lancashire coalfield beyond Warrington or of the coastal belt from Liverpool northwards. Inside the flat belts of West and North-west Lancashire there are several isolated pieces of country that are worthy of more than a passing glance, notably around **Parbold**, at the mouths of the **River Wyre** and **River Lune** and in the vicinity of **Silverdale** and **Arnside**.

All these lie close to the main roads running northwards from the River Mersey, and merit the cyclist's attention. Parbold and the flat district between A6 and the seaboard may be visited with advantage from **Southport**, a large and rather 'select' seaside resort some miles north of Liverpool, and partly a dormitory for the Merseyside city. The estuaries of the Wyre and Lune are within day-riding distance of Blackpool and Morecambe, while in the farthest north of the three belts, along the north-eastern side of Morecambe Bay, the principal cause of the scenic variety is an outcrop of carboniferous limestone, seen at its best in the rocky ridges of **Arnside Knott** and **Farleton Knott**.

The **Mersey Tunnel**, opened in 1933, provides a road link between the Wirral Peninsula, at Birkenhead, Cheshire, and Liverpool, in Lancashire. The tunnel is for vehicular traffic only, including bicycles, has four traffic lines, and is 170 ft. below high-water at its deepest point. The roadway through the tunnel has a surface of iron set in concrete, the longest iron road in the world—two miles of it all told.

Leave Liverpool by Scotland Road, and pass through Seaforth (note the overhead railway on the left), Great and Little Crosby, and Formby, along a busy road that keeps well away from the sea. Beyond Ainsdale comes Birkdale, and the suburbs of Southport are entered. (Liverpool to Southport—20 miles.)

Lord Street, in Southport, is built like a boulevard, while the resort itself has far more trees and gardens than elsewhere on the Lancashire coast, together with a marine drive and a pier 1,400 yds. long that has a railway to the sea—the tide goes out a long way at Southport!

NOTE. Some 12 miles east of Southport and reached by lanes through Burscough and Newburgh, is the village of **Parbold**, on the edge of the Lancashire coalfield. There are rocky outcrops here, while to the south-west stands **Lathom House** and Park, the former on the site of old Lathom House, where, in 1643, Lady Lathom and a small band held out against the Parliamentarians. Over high ground running south-east from Parbold, the village of Upholland can be gained. A little east of the village a footpath commences and runs northwards with a stream through **Dean Wood**, a delightful cycle run of about two sylvan miles, emerging finally near Gathurst Station, whence Parbold can be regained via Shevington.

From Southport the main road to Preston goes across marshlands, never approaching the mudflats of the Ribble estuary. (Liverpool to Preston, via Southport—39 miles.) Preston has little to show the cyclist, but it is an historic town close to the lowest bridges across the Ribble. At **Walton-le-Dale**, a village south of the Ribble on A6, is the Unicorn Inn, long condemned to be destroyed, but still serving as a rendezvous for cyclists, particularly for the Northern old-timers' organization called 'The Autumn Tints', to which Tom Hughes, intrepid Wigan tourist, belongs.

The Preston-Blackpool road is busy with cars and coaches for most of the year. For a somewhat quieter route, turn off the main road some four miles west of Preston and go across Freckleton Marsh to the dignified resort of Lytham and its smaller neighbour, St. Annes. At Squires Gate, entering Blackpool and amid the sandhills, is a large camping site. **Blackpool** (Preston-Blackpool, via Lytham—21; 17 direct) is a bustling resort that has 'everything'— except trees!

A built-up road leads northwards by Bispham to Cleveleys and Rossall, close to an enclosed tramway route, with low, crumbly cliffs to the west. **Fleetwood**, the largest fishing port on the west coast of England, is a resort where prices are reasonable. It is also one of the main ports for the Isle of Man. (Blackpool to Fleetwood—9½ miles). A regular vehicular ferry runs across the mouth of the River Wyre to Knott End, the finish of a former light railway from Garstang. Pleasant lanes lead across the levels by Preesall and Pilling and across Pilling Sands (liable to flooding), breezy and haunted by marsh birds, to the whitewashed hamlet of Cockerham, where turn left towards Lancaster on a better road. Just before the bridge at Conder Green a lane runs leftwards to **Glasson Dock**, a deserted spot, used nowadays by a few pleasure boats. To the south is **Cockersand Abbey**, founded in 1190 and with only the chapter-house remaining. The run into Lancaster by Conder Green is less interesting, but grey stone walls by the roadside denote that the levels are being left and the hard, craggy hills of the north approached. (Blackpool to Lancaster—25 miles.)

The bridge across the Lune, north of Lancaster, takes A6 closer to the coast than at any point on its course from London to Carlisle. Beyond Slyne the shores of Morecambe Bay can be seen to the left and, across the wide stretch of sand and water, the Lakeland mountains begin to appear. Hest Bank, a little to the south-west, was formerly the start of the 'over-sands' route to Kent's Bank, a much-used way, but treacherous owing to the shifting streams and sands. Guides could be hired for the journey, which saved many miles of road. At Bolton-le-Sands, which is not exactly by the sea, there are lanes that lead leftwards to grassy camp sites close to the Bay.

The next large place is **Carnforth**, important once for its blast furnaces and still busy as the junction of the old Furness Railway with the former L.N.W.R. and Midland systems. Leave the main road here for a lane that runs west of **Warton Crag**, through hilly country, to the scattered village of Silverdale. There are fine woods hereabouts, and all the limestone hills show the typical 'desk' formation of the district.

The road to Arnside enters Westmorland at **Elmslack**, passes on the right the ruins of **Arnside Tower**, and then climbs the side of the Red Hills before dropping to the sea shore and the houses of **Arnside**. (Lancaster to Arnside—14 miles.)

NOTE. An alternative route to Arnside is found by turning off the main road, passing the farm of Far Arnside, and then going by a narrow, rough lane through woods to the farm of New Barns (camp sites) and along the low, rocky cliffs to Arnside.

The whole area east of Silverdale and Arnside to A6 is worth exploration. Notable are the 30 acres of **Hawes Water** (not to be confused with Manchester's reservoir near Penrith), a fresh-water lake with a depth in places of 100 ft. On a knoll close by is the **Buckstone**, a great boulder, estimated to weigh 60 tons, and a relic of the Ice Age. 'The Fairy Steps' make another short excursion. A little farther away is **Yealand Conyers**, set on a hillside and a stronghold of the Society of Friends.

A handy way of crossing the estuary of the River Kent where it meets Morecambe Bay is by railway across the bridge and into

Grange-over-Sands, a Lancashire resort with a rocky hinterland, looking south-eastwards across the bay.

The road route round to Grange goes by the seashore to Sandside and then to A6 at **Milnthorpe**, turning left theRe for **Leven's Bridge**, where left again and across the mosses by **Gilpin's Bridge** to Lindale and Grange, a distance of some 14 miles.

There is some tourist accommodation at Grange, but less pretentious quarters may be had at **Cartmel** (2 miles west), where there is a fine priory church, with a square belfry believed to be unique. There is also a 14th century gabled gatehouse overlooking a quaint village square which has also an ancient cross. The village is set in a quiet countryside, where clear streams flow down from high ridges. Cartmel makes a good jumping-off place for the remote valleys and moorlands of southern Lakeland. (Arnside to Cartmel, using the railway from Arnside to Grange—2 miles.)

LUNEDALE
(Lancaster to Shap, via Tebay—50 miles)

The **Valley of the River Lune**, from Lancaster to near its source above Tebay, provides one of the most entrancing of all gateways to the north country. Most of it is quiet and rarely visited, and it provides a pleasant alternative route to the main A6 road over Shap Fell. The scenery varies from the rich riverside beauty of '**The Crook o' Lune**' to the wild, austere fells around **Tebay** and Orton. The gorge of the upper Lune between **Lowgill** and Tebay (a glimpse of which is obtained from the main L.M.S. line between Euston and Glasgow) is as fine a valley picture as can be found in the district. Accommodation is not plentiful, however, except at **Kirkby Lonsdale**, and the only suitable youth hostel lies 10 miles off the route at Cowgill, above Dent.

On the whole, of the two roads up Lunedale, the one on the south and east side of the river is to be preferred. The exit from Lancaster by the riverside road is not prepossessing, but before **Caton**, some five miles out, the delightful bend in the stream called 'The Crook o' Lune' is encountered. The banks may be approached more closely afoot. After crossing the River Wenning, a tributary from the east, **Hornby** is entered. As seen from the bridge, the view is characteristically English. Low hills and green fields, old stone houses, a castle and a church are all in the scene. In the churchyard is the base of a Saxon cross, while to the left of the road, going north, is tree-covered **Castle Stede**, a mound and ditch signifying the former presence of a motte and bailey stronghold.

The road continues through the broad valley, passing the rural villages of **Melling** and **Tunstall**.

NOTE. From Nether Barrow, a little over a mile north of Tunstall, a lane leads rightwards into Cowan Bridge, where there was formerly a school for clergymen's daughters, brought vividly to life in the early pages of Jane Eyre. The school has been broken up into cottages. Above Leek, close to Cowan Bridge, an upland lane climbs the side of Leek Fell, finishing on the open moors, and giving access to **Lost John's Cave**, an intricate 'pot' that should not be entered without an expert guide. To the right of the track is **Ease Gill**, a limestone watercourse, while farther on is Bull Pot. From the latter a track drops to Blindbeck Bridge, in Barbondale, between Barbon and Dent.

From either Nether Burrow or Leek main highways go in 2 miles to **Devil's Bridge**, which formerly carried the main Skipton-Kendal road across the Lune. The old bridge is now superseded by a modern structure. It got its name from an encounter that the Prince of Darkness had with a wily old woman. He promised that he would build a bridge for her if he could have the soul of the first living creature to cross. The old woman agreed, and drove a hen over as she made her first dry-shod crossing! The narrow stone bridge is picturesquely situated on a grand reach of the river. **Kirkby Lonsdale**, less than a mile to the north-west, is handy for bed and breakfast or for meals. (Lancaster to Kirkby Lonsdale—18 miles.)

Beyond Devil's Bridge the valley narrows and the hills rise boldly to the right in a series of graceful and individual fells. This is Westmorland, and although the valley has its fat pastures, the influence of the hills is over all. The villages are of stone and wear a comfortable, settled look. They are also less frequent, and between Casterton and Middleton there are five miles in which roadside habitations are few.

NOTE. From **Barbon**, a village just off the road halfway between Casterton and Middleton, a romantic lane-route leads through Barbondale in some six miles to Dent, close to which is a youth hostel. The descent on Gawthorp, near Dent, however, is steep and winding, and should be walked after dark. The route is really done best in reverse, from Dent to Barbon.

At a fork beyond **Middleton** the way is rightwards into **Sedbergh**. (See page 61.) (Kirkby Lonsdale to Sedbergh—12 miles.)

From Sedbergh retrace the route a short way and continue up Lunedale along a narrow lane running along the west side of the valley.

NOTE. A sporting alternative, less hilly but rough, runs along the east of the valley, emerging at **Low Borrow Bridge**. 'Rough stuff' enthusiasts will prefer this route. One branch commences in Sedbergh, the other close to the Lune Bridge, two miles west on the road described above. The branches join in the hills north of Sedbergh Station.

There is a hard climb beyond the high station of **Lowgill** (note the masonry of the railway viaducts), and then a terrace which gives splendid views of the rounded fells and the sparkling river below, leads to a sudden fall to **Low Borrow Bridge**, where the scenery reaches its finest level, the bold fells hemming in the narrow valley. The route continues into **Tebay**, a busy railway junction, and then climbs steadily into the upland, reaching the scattered village of **Orton**, a farming community amidst the fells. (Sedbergh to Orton—12 miles.)

From Orton the road becomes rough and crosses open moorland, climbing to **Shap Thorn**, where A6 is met some three miles south of **Shap** village. (Orton to Shap village—8 miles.)

NOTE. This route, between Sedbergh and Shap, forms a useful connection between the Yorkshire Dales and the Lake District. From Shap village a lane descends to Bampton, at the foot of Haweswater, and from there, there is a link with the foot of **Ullswater**, at **Pooley Bridge**, through **Askham**.

THE PENNINE LINK
(Glossop to Addingham—71 miles)

The tourist who has spent a few days in Derbyshire and wishes to reach the Yorkshire Dales or the Lake District, faces a fairly complex problem if he desires to avoid the industrialism of south-east Lancashire on the one hand and that of the West Riding on the other. The sensible way is to take to the Pennines, 'the backbone of England,' that separates the two areas.

The Pennines, even taken from south to north, provide a formidable barrier. However, a compromise route is possible for the tourist who does not wish to hurry and who wants to get a lasting impression of any district through which he travels. The accommodation on this route is infrequent, but there are youth hostels at Wood Cottage, 2½ miles west of Holmfirth, and on the road, and also at Wainstalls and Mankinholes, near Hebden Bridge.

The starting point is the Derbyshire manufacturing town of **Glossop**, some 15 miles from **Buxton**, by the hilly road through Chapel-en-le-Frith and Hayfield.

From Glossop the road northwards leads over a low hill into the **Longdendale Valley**, a cleft in the high, black moorlands that has been filled with reservoirs and all their attendant works. For once, these artificial sheets of water are not out of keeping with their surroundings, and strike a bright note in a sombre setting. Beyond Crowden Station (on the L.N.E.R. line—formerly Great Central—between Manchester and London, Marylebone) the valley is crossed by the embankment of Woodhead Reservoir. Then the hamlet of **Woodhead** is entered at tiny Woodhead Church on its rocky hillock.

NOTE. A mile or two west, at Crowden village, commences the severe route—for experienced pass-stormers only—over by Laddow Rocks to Chew Reservoir, the Chew Brook and Greenfield. The path runs along the west side of the Crowden Great Brook, climbs steeply past Laddow Rocks, traverses the boggy gullies south of Black Chew Head, follows the south bank of Chew Reservoir—said to be the highest in England—and then falls roughly down the north-east side of the Chew Brook into Greenfield, on the Manchester-Holmfirth road. The crossing takes about three hours, and should not be attempted in mist or bad weather.

From Woodhead Church the main valley road is followed rightwards to the fork at the Woodhead Inn, where a 'skull and crossbones' warning formerly gave—and may still give—a grim warning of the hazards of the road that comes next. The way is left, around an Alpine saucer of a bend at **Heyden Bridge**, after which the highway climbs sharply for nearly two miles on a shelf above the Heyden Brook. The summit of the road is 1,725 ft. above sea-level. Looking southwards at Holme Moss, the eye ranges, beyond the Woodhead rift, along the great unpathed moorland massif of **Bleaklow**, the loneliest tract in Britain south of the Cheviots. Northwards the ridges pile their shoulders amongst the smoke pall of the Yorkshire woollen towns.

The descent is steep to **Holme** and again to Holmbridge, after which comes a mile of relatively level going into **Holmfirth**. This is a district that is liable to sudden flooding, and more than one disaster has occurred owing to the sudden onrush of the waters from the hill streams. Holmfirth is a typical valley town of the industrial West Riding, a busy, unpretentious place of stone, with rows of houses strung out in terraces along the hillsides or climbing steeply uphill. (Glossop to Holmfirth—13 miles.)

A hairpin leftwards in the centre of Holmfirth takes the tourist up a steady climb (passing the youth hostel) that emerges in 4½ miles on to the open moor at the **Isle of Skye Inn**, a grim-looking hostelry standing four-square to all the winds that blow. The inn is the fourth highest in England. (See table on page 43.)

An adventurous, but quite practicable, shortcut, saving some three miles, turns off at Holmbridge, and goes by Austonley, joining the Holmfirth-Isle of Skye road at the Ford Inn, not far from the youth hostel at Wood Cottage mentioned above.

Just east of the inn a side road goes downhill steeply in the direction of Meltham and Huddersfield. A short way along this road, however, a track turns leftwards into a deep hollow in which there are reservoirs. This is the **Wessenden Valley**, filled with the waterworks of the Huddersfield Corporation, yet giving one of the grandest impressions of this gritstone district. The track keeps to the eastern flanks and hangs mostly on precipitous hillsides, now and again diving sharply to narrow wooden bridges across tributary streams, where the nervous would be well advised to walk. At Wessenden Lodge there may be a possibility of a cup of tea, and thereafter the road, while still spectacular, is broader and runs down into the industrial centre of **Marsden**. (Holmfirth to Marsden—9 miles.)

NOTE. From Marsden a track runs north-westward, along the north side of the River Colne at first, climbing, after crossing an ancient pack-horse bridge, to the moorlands and emerging on the Outlane (Huddersfield)-Denshaw (Oldham) road, whence it is a long, smooth fall into Denshaw. (See continuation of main route.) About 2½ hours are needed for the journey from Marsden to Denshaw, as much of the way is quite unrideable.

From Marsden two roads run south-westwards towards Delph. The main road climbs steadily, but the alternative, starting close to the foot of the Wessenden Valley, is quieter and shorter. The routes rejoin two miles from Marsden, on Standedge. This is one of the most important of the main Pennine crossings by road, but hardly the most impressive, as the moorlands are dingy and the stone houses lacking in character. The summit of the pass—which is much used by heavy lorry traffic—is marked by a cutting, beyond which the road descends, past an inn with the strange name of 'The Floating Light', into New Delph. At the crossroads here the way is right to **Delph** (meaning 'a quarry'), a townlet of tall houses and steep streets in the true mountain tradition. From Delph the road mounts to **Denshaw** (locally known as 'Junction' from the inn at the meeting of five main roads), a small village shielded by a range of hills to the east from the nearby Lancashire cotton towns. Hereabouts there are cottages and inns providing teas or 'tea only' the latter being a Lancashire and Yorkshire institution for those carrying their own food. (Marsden to Denshaw—9 miles.)

NOTE. A shorter but more industrialized and rougher alternative—better in bad weather—commences at Denshaw. This first climbs steeply to the Moorcock Inn, and then descends into Newhey, where the way is right into Milnrow, At the foot of the village a road—Kiln Lane—climbs rightwards. At the hilltop inn the way is leftwards along a lane that leads to a red-brick hospital, beyond which the route turns right and then left along the north-west bank of **Hollingworth Lake**, a former canal reservoir, greatly frequented in summer for boating. There are catering houses hereabouts. At an inn called 'The Fisherman's Rest', the way is left into **Littleborough**, where after a canal bank section the road goes left under a railway arch, and then immediately right along the Todmorden road. Beyond Summit the road improves and runs through a deep valley, industrialized in its later stages, into **Todmorden**, where the way is right, down the Calder Valley to **Hebden Bridge**. The youth hostel at Mankinholes lies to the right, as well as the prominent tower of Stoodley Pike. (Denshaw-Hebden Bridge—18 miles.)

From Denshaw the main route goes uphill, rising to fine, sweeping moorland country. There is a steady drop subsequently, with a deepening vale to the right, past the **Derby Bar Inn**, reaching, some six miles from Denshaw, the bend named Cunning Corner. The valley becomes wooded and deeper at Rishworth, after which it reaches **Ripponden**. (Note the similarity between this section and the one immediately preceding Holmfirth.)

In the middle of Ripponden the route hairpins leftwards towards Rochdale, rising steeply to the open moors again.

NOTE. From the Derby Bar Inn a lane climbs leftwards and runs on the edge of the moorland to Baitings Gate, more than halfway between Ripponden and the summit of the crossing.

This is **Blackstone Edge**, the hill crossing that so scared Daniel Defoe. As the final rise to the summit commences, and when the last moorland clough can be seen ascending to the left not far from the road, the bicycle should be hidden in the moorgrass and a walk undertaken to one of the finest remaining Roman relics in England, a causeway that has withstood the ravages of 1,800 years.

Traces of the road can be picked up in the clough, but the bridge is a restoration, a piece of work done voluntarily by unemployed men from Rochdale and district during the depression of the early 1930s. The pavement, of large pieces of worked gritstone, can be seen close to the bridge, where a smooth face of living rock was also used for the surface. The course of the Roman road can be traced by walking over the ridge. In places the causeway disappears, only to re-appear again. It is worthwhile descending from the ridge down the west (or Lancashire side), as there is an easily visible stretch of road rising above the peaty moorland, not far from a heap of stones, which has been identified as the remains of a small fort. The curious hollow down the centre of the road has been the subject of speculation amongst antiquarians. Some hold that its sole purpose was as a drain, but others are certain that it represents the scoring action of a pole brake used by the Romans as their wagons and chariots descended the slope. From the Lancashire side there is a wide view—when the absence of smoke permits—across the upper valley of the River Roch. The prominent rocks along the ridge to the south are called **Robin Hood's Bed**, from a legend that the famous outlaw once hid there. To-day they provide mild and safe rock-climbing exercise.

Returning to the bicycle, follow the road through a cutting until it passes (briefly) into Lancashire and reaches a sign-post by the side of a reservoir. Here the way is rightwards (into Yorkshire again), and down **Cragg Vale**. This is probably the longest *continuous* descent in England, nearly six miles in all, and a fair recompense for the climbing done previously. Once again the valley exhibits the usual Pennine characteristics, a small hollow, amidst the wild moors deepening and forming a richly wooded clough.

At **Mytholmroyd** the way is left along the Calder Valley to **Hebden Bridge**, where begins the climb of four miles by Pecket Well to **Cock Hill** (1,400 ft.). Then go downhill, taking the greatest care on two hairpin bends near the foot of the descent, into **Oxenhope**. **Haworth** (see page 119) lies to left, across the valley. Beyond **Cross Roads** another descent leads into **Keighley**, a manufacturing town in Airedale. Continue through the town and follow Airedale past Utley to **Steeton**. Leave the Skipton road to the left, in favour of the Silsden road to the right. **Silsden** is a small industrial townlet, and beyond it the route climbs for nearly two miles to the summit of **Cringles Hill**. From this point it drops into **Addingham**, where the greatest care should be exercised on entering the main street at the foot of the hill.

Addingham is three miles south of **Bolton Abbey**, and within reach of **Ilkley** (4½ miles), from which the youth hostel at Burley Wood Head may be reached by a road on the edge of **Ilkley Moor**, and **Otley** (9 miles), on the way to the Great North Road at **Wetherby** and to **Harrogate** via Pool.

The famous '**Ilkla Moor**' of the song lies south of the interesting Wharfedale town of Ilkley, which has an old bridge and some Saxon crosses in the churchyard. High above the town, to the south, are the **Cow and Calf Rocks**, claimed as having some resemblance to these bovine creatures. There is a rough, steep, but tolerable, road southwards across Ilkley Moor by Keighley Gate to Riddlesden.

The best viewpoint in Lower Wharfedale, however, is **The Chevin**, a rocky outcrop on a ridge south of Otley, and easily approached on foot from that town. The prospect extends not only up and down the rich valley of the Wharfe, but also up the **Washburn Valley**, with its string of reservoirs, and eastwards across the Plain of York. As with so many other viewpoints, it is claimed that from The Chevin York Minster can be seen. Near **Chevin End**, at the west side of the ridge, stands the old-established Menston Clarion Clubhouse. (Denshaw to Addingham—40 miles.)

Shorter Tours and Connecting Routes today

The 169-mile **Way of the Roses** has really helped boost cycling in Lancashire, which now hosts three major routes of the National Cycle Network. The Way of the Roses is based on sections of various National Route numbers in Lancashire. It snakes east from Morecambe largely on minor roads and travels right through the **Forest of Bowland** before scaling some serious climbs and descents when entering the Yorkshire Dales.

National Route 6 runs north to south through **Lancaster** itself on a canal path then on to a converted railway path south of the city. The route has been completed between **Kendal** and **Preston**, a distance of around 55 miles.

There is also the **Lancashire Cycleway** or **Regional Routes 90 and 91**, which is made up of two giant loops and totals a heady 260 miles. Highlights of this beautiful ride include traversing the **Forest of Bowland** (Area of Natural Beauty) on the north loop and exploring the **West Pennine Moors** on the southern loop.

Useful maps and books (available from www.sustransshop.co.uk): *Way of the Roses Cycle Route Map; The Lancashire Cycleway* (Cicerone guide book).

PART V

DAY AND WEEK-END TOURS

THE WESTERN EDGE OF THE PLAIN OF YORK
(Addingham to Richmond—52½ miles)

THE large village of **Addingham**, in Wharfedale, can be made the start of a short tour that serves as a link between the Pennine country described in the previous section, and the dales and moors north of Richmond, extending through the Durham dales to the Roman Wall, the Cheviots and the Scottish Border.

Some three miles north of Addingham is **Bolton Abbey** (previously mentioned), a mile beyond the village of Bolton Bridge, more noteworthy for its situation beside the clear waters of the River Wharfe than for its own intrinsic beauty. The abbey is placed on a green sward and beyond the curving river rise low, wood-feathered hills. The abbey was founded in the 12th century for monks of the Order of St. Augustine, although the original site was at Embsay, closer to Skipton. The nave was re-roofed in 1864, while the choir, the north transepts and a wall of the south transepts remain in ruins. An Iona Cross in the north-west corner of the churchyard, and the Cavendish Fountain, on a little hill close to the main Wharfedale road, a little north of the abbey, commemorate Lord Frederick Cavendish, Chief Secretary to Ireland, who was assassinated in Phoenix Park, Dublin, on May 6, 1882.

The main route recommended is identical with that to Bolton Abbey as far as **Bolton Bridge**. Here, however, it turns rightwards, across the bridge spanning the River Wharfe, and then climbs steadily alongside the Kex Beck to the summit of the main Harrogate road, at 949 ft.

Here, however, where the main road swings rightwards and begins to descend, the way is left along a narrow moorland highway that climbs for another 50 ft. before swinging into an upland hollow. Thereafter the lane undulates steeply past Thruscross and Padside through fine open country, emerging on a better-surfaced road at Dacre, from which, by turning leftwards, the village of

Summerbridge, in Nidderdale, is reached. (Addingham to Summerbridge—14 miles.)

Straight ahead a steep lane mounts to the boulder-strewn upland of Brimham Moor. Some two miles above Summerbridge, **Brimharn Rocks** can be seen on the left. There is a small charge for admission to view the gritstone fantasies of Brimham. From afar the scene can be likened to that of a heavily blitzed city, but closer examination reveals that the dark, heathy waste is strewn with huge boulders and blocks, first cleft by earth convulsions and later weathered into their various shapes, many of which have been given fanciful names. From the Rocks there is a good view of Nidderdale beyond Pateley Bridge, and also eastwards across the Plain of York. On occasion the conical tip of Roseberry Topping, far to the north-east, can be seen, and also the wall-like south-western face of the Hambleton Hills south of it. The spires of York Minster are within sight, too.

Beyond Brimham Rocks the narrow highway wanders northwards, passing a dark plantation, until it meets the Pateley Bridge-Ripon road.

NOTE. In a little mote than a mile to the east a lane drops into the village of Sawley. Beyond the church a wooded side road runs downhill through a valley to **Fountains Abbey**. The abbey and the nearby grounds of **Studley Royal** are worth exploration, for the ruins are amongst the finest in the north of England. Particularly outstanding is the Lady Chapel or Chapel of the Nine Altars, a fine example of Early English architecture. At the time of writing (January, 1947), there is a project afoot to restore the Abbey and make it a Roman Catholic establishment. This proposition is, however, being opposed in some quarters.

The tourist not diverging to see Fountains should continue past the first Sawley fork, go left and then cross the River Skell at some particularly charming parkland west of Grantley Hall. The lane goes over the crossroads at the village of High Grantley, and after a slope downwards and a left turn, enters the large village of **Kirkby**

Malzeard, close to a large restored church at the east end of the place. Here there is a youth hostel of the old, simpler and friendlier type, quite close to the church. (Summerbridge to Kirkby Malzeard—10 miles.)

NOTE. West of Kirkby Malzeard, on the edge of the moorland some three miles away, is the gorge of **Dallowgill**, a rarely visited valley that deserves close examination. It can be approached by bicycle through Laverton, but the gill itself must be explored afoot.

Proceeding northwards from Kirkby Malzeard, and a little beyond the quaint village of Grewelthorpe, the road dips to a tiny beck that flows rightwards into the winding River Yore, at **Hack Fall**. A small charge is made for admission to the grounds, and the bicycle must be left behind. The 'fall' as such is negligible, the beck providing no more than a trickle. The real quest is for the ravine scenery where the stream enters the River Yore. The finest view point lies leftwards at a corner called Mowbray Point. The banks are wooded and steep, and between them the river runs in a turmoil along its rocky course.

From the entrance to Hack Fall the roadway descends through open country to the little town of **Masham** (pronounced *Mass-*ham). There is a large market-place here and an interesting church, with Norman work in the lower part of its imposing tower.

NOTE A lane runs eastwards from Masham, crossing the Yore and climbing over a ridge to meet the Great North Road at Sinderby Station, some eight miles from Masham.

Beyond Masham the Yore valley widens and past the outskirts of High Ellington descends close to the river at the entrance to Jervaulx Park.

Through a gateway on the right the precincts of **Jervaulx Abbey** can be entered (small charge). There is little to see except the foundations and a few ruined arches and pillars. The whole place is, however, very neatly kept.

The road up the dale next approaches **East Witton**, swinging off rightwards to cross the Yore at Cover Bridge.

NOTE. About 3½ miles west of East Witton, and gained by a lane that runs along a shelf commanding a wide prospect across Wensleydale, stand the scanty remains of Coverham Abbey. From the village of Coverham a moorland route runs south-westwards to Carlton, and the crossing by Park Rash to Kettlewell described on page 59.

From East Witton the dales road goes in 2 miles to **Middleham**. This is one of the finest of Yorkshire's little towns. It stands on a slope above the River Yore, and has the usual wide market-place of these parts. The castle is the outstanding feature. It is really two buildings in one, a Norman keep surrounded by an outer ring of later buildings, which were added by the powerful Neville family. The walls of the keep are nine feet thick. Edward IV was held a prisoner here by Warwick, 'the Kingmaker'.

Lovers of horses will find much to interest them around Middleham, for the breezy heathland around the townlet is used for exercising racehorses from the successful stables in the district. (Kirkby-Malzeard to Middleham—14 miles.)

From Middleham, still going north-west, the road crosses the Yore. Less than half a mile onwards the lane leftwards into **Wensley** should be taken. The village, placed on a slant and with a pretty little green, gives its name to Wensleydale (of which the river is the Yore or Ure), and also to a particularly satisfying brand of cheese. Wensleydale is perhaps the most gracious of all the Yorkshire Dales.

NOTE. From Wensley a lane runs along the northern bank of the Yore, and in three miles reaches the village of Redmire, west of which is the hamlet of Castle Bolton and **Bolton Castle**, a bold keep a little westward, which commands the dale. It is square and without pretensions to beauty. The castle was built by Lord Chancellor Scrope in the time of Richard II. The royalists held it in the Civil War, but were forced to surrender. Earlier, Mary Queen of Scots was held at Bolton.

The castle consists of three great towers connected by stout walls.

From Wensley, going north-east, **Leyburn** is entered. This neat townlet, around an open square, makes a handy base for Wensleydale. Its chief claim to fame is its proximity to **The Shawl**, a long ridge running westwards in a terrace that commands a fine view of the richest part of the valley. It is approached (on foot) from the upper end of the town square. Halfway along the terrace is the Queen's Gap, so called because it was the point, according to a legend, where Mary Queen of Scots was stopped during an escape attempt from Bolton Castle. The view is full of variety. Below, the Yore flows through a gentle valley, Middleham can be seen as a prominent feature of the landscape and in the distance the land rises to the moors of the south and south-west. The boldest hill in view is **Penhill Beacon** (1,685 ft.) a jutting neb of moorland noticeable beyond Wensley.

Continuing along the road northwards a climb leads to the village of Bellerby and beyond that to the road junction of Halfpenny House.

NOTE. From this part a road runs directly across Downholme Moor to Richmond, but it is inferior to the highway by the River Swale, and is liable to closure by the military.

Beyond Halfpenny House the route goes downhill through woodlands to join Swaledale at one of its most romantic reaches. Onwards towards Richmond the whole scene is delightful. The road first runs on a ledge on the south bank of the Swale, crossing the river at Swale Bridge, a lovely corner. The woods climb steeply from the water's edge, and the Swale, still a mountain stream, dashes impetuously over its rocky bed.

As **Richmond** is entered along the north bank, the road becomes suburbanized. The town is ranged around the square, in which stands the Trinity Church, which has shops under its roof, in the mediaeval fashion. Close by is the restored market cross. The castle consists of a fine keep and is well situated high above the River Swale. It was formerly one of the strongest fortresses in England. The keep dates back to A.D. 1150. The castle can be visited for a small charge.

Rather more than a mile from Richmond is **Easby Abbey**, reached by a riverside walk. The ruins are beautifully situated but scanty, the chief remaining feature being a Norman arch on the west side. South-east of the Abbey stands the little parish church of Easby, an unconventional structure dating from the end of the 12th century.

Richmond makes an admirable jumping off place for Swaledale (westwards), Teesdale (north-westwards) and the Cleveland Hills (eastwards). Beyond **Gilling**, to the north, the road running from Scotch Corner and the Great North Road by Bowes and Bowes Moor to Brough, Appleby and Penrith, to Carlisle—one of the great highways into Scotland—can be joined. (Middleham to Richmond—14½ miles.)

POOL TO RICHMOND

A faster road to Richmond, over main roads, and closer to the Plain of York, starts at Pool, some ten miles north of Leeds and Bradford. Crossing the River Wharfe, the road climbs for 8½ miles into Harrogate, formerly the scene of great C.T.C. meets. The town covers a large area, many of its buildings being placed around the 200-acre 'Stray,' an open space.

Some four miles east of Harrogate is **Knaresborough**, a favourite resort with cyclists, in a picturesque situation on the River Nidd. The town itself is old-world, and includes the remains of a castle on a lofty crest of sandstone. John Metcalfe, or 'Blind Jack,' was a local celebrity who attained wide fame in the early part of the 18th century for his road- and bridge-making. Despite his affliction, he made a name as a gallant, partly as the result of an episode in which he eloped with a woman on what should have been the eve of her marriage with a rival! Steps lead down from the castle to the riverside—here the limestone caps the sandstone—and then leftwards to the Mother Shipton Inn, named in memory of a celebrated local seer who foresaw motorcars and aeroplanes. Not far away is the Dropping Well, where objects are petrified by the action of the impregnated water.

Continuing along the road northwards from Harrogate, there is little to hold the tourist until **Ripley**, where the Nidd is crossed. The village is an attractive one with a set of stocks and an old church.

The road continues to undulate until Ripon is reached—19 miles from Pool, 10½ from Harrogate, 32 from York, 9 from Thirsk, 13 from Pateley Bridge.

The Swale at Easby Abbey

Ripon is a neat city that is a favourite rendezvous for cyclists. Its oblong market square, to the south of which is the Town Hall, has in its centre an obelisk named The Cross, erected in 1781 to replace an older one. The cathedral, on a site first occupied in the 7th century, is not, however, of great beauty. The Early English west front is notable. The nave is 270 ft. long.

From Ripon, the easiest road to Richmond drops to the River Yore, passing the station and crossing agricultural land to Baldersby Gate, on Leeming Lane, part of the Great North Road, A1.

The road is straight and there is little to call for a halt until Catterick Bridge, beyond which a left turn leads by Terrace Road, a fine entrance into **Richmond**—45 miles from Pool.

CLOSE TO THE TOWNS

One feature of touring in northern England that will not have escaped the reader's notice is how frequently certain areas close to industrial districts are full of interest to cyclists and to other appreciative travellers. In concluding the first volume of this series, the writer will try to indicate a few of the minor regions, mostly (but not entirely) within a day's or week-end's range of the large Lancashire and Yorkshire towns.

THE WASHBURN VALLEY

North of Otley, in Wharfedale, some ten miles from Leeds and Bradford, is to be found the comparative backwater of the Washburn Valley. The scenery presented is typically Pennine, a dun-tinted waste of upland, diversified in its hollows by evergreen plantations and the sheets of reservoirs.

There is no regular road up the valley, but a route from Otley by Farnley Park and Farnley, crossing the Washburn to the eastern slope and then going left along a ledge lane past Folly Hall to Jack Hill, Bland Hill and the scattered fellside village of **Fewston**, leads to **Blubberhouses** on the Harrogate-Bolton Bridge highway.

From Blubberhouses a fine moorland lane runs north-westward past Humberstone Bank and Palleys Crags to **Greenhow** village, on the bleak uplands between Pateley Bridge and Grassington. There are caves near Greenhow, while the descent eastwards to Pateley Bridge by **Greenhow Hill** is one of the most famous in Yorkshire.

YORKSHIRE 'SIGHTS'

The county of Yorkshire is one of the most remarkable in the whole of England for its 'sights', places that are worth a divergence from a through route and fit objectives for a day run by a club. Many of these show-places were mentioned in earlier chapters, but there are far more than can be brought within the scope of this work. Some, however, cannot be overlooked.

Typical of the gems to be found in the industrialized West Riding is **Kirkstall Abbey**, the ruins of which stand close to the sullied waters of the Aire. The surroundings of the Abbey must have been remote and well wooded before the factories and forges were built. Kirkstall is, after Fountains Abbey, the most complete in Yorkshire. It was founded *circa* A.D. 1150, and the ruins cover a considerable area. The abbey is situated about three miles north-west of Leeds.

Five miles north of Leeds, about two miles from Headingley, stands the little Norman church of **Adel**, 500 ft. above sea level. It was founded in the 12th century, and was dedicated to St. John the Baptist. It has been restored with due care.

About half a mile east of Boroughbridge, an old-fashioned townlet on the Great North Road, north of Wetherby, are to be found the **Devil's Arrows**, three gritstone pillars standing in a field. They are 200-300 ft. apart, and stand about 20 ft. high. Their origin and purpose can only be conjectured.

Nine miles west of Rotherham and eight miles east of Bawtry (on the Great North Road) are to be found, down a side turning on the edge of a colliery district, the remains of **Roche Abbey**, an offshoot of Fountains. There is not a great deal to see, but the stumps of handsome clustered pillars are to be noted.

Some five miles west of the large mining and railway centre of Doncaster lies **Conisbrough Castle**, of which Scott wrote in *Ivanhoe*. The district is murky now, but there is no mistaking the strength of the position of the castle overlooking the River Don. Two round towers and a keep, the latter with walls 15 ft. thick and supporting buttresses, are noteworthy features. The castle dates from the 12th century.

Pontefract, for all its importance as a mining centre, still looks as if it had a history. The interest is centred on Pontefract Castle, founded soon after the Conquest by de Lacy, a Norman baron. The building had a chequered history right down to the Civil War. The ruins stand on a rock, and consist of a strong keep approached by stairs and out works. From the Round Tower there is an extensive view.

Wakefield, on the polluted River Calder, is to Yorkshire as Wigan is to Lancashire—an ancient town in the centre of an old coalfield. All Saints Parish Church includes a chancel arch believed to be a relic of a church built in 1329. The present church was built mostly in the 15th century, and is Perpendicular in style. More worth of passing note, however, is the Chantry Church, a fine Perpendicular building on the old bridge over the Calder, one of the few bridge churches remaining in England. The church and bridge date from the reign of Edward III, but the former has since been restored. The bridge has been by-passed by a new structure, and can only be crossed on foot.

The village of **Cawthorne**, about five miles west of Barnsley, and situated in the characteristic hill and dale scenery of the Pennines, is a delightful place with an old church. The gritstone houses on the edge of the moorlands are in the Bronte tradition of stateliness next door to the wild.

Two or three miles south of Huddersfield is the village of **Almondbury,** close to which is Castle Hill, whereon stands a tower that commands a wide view over the folds and vales of the West Riding woollen district.

FROM YORKSHIRE TO WALES

The rider making for North Wales from the West Riding is confronted with the difficulty of crossing industrial south Lancashire. Riders from Leeds, Bradford and Halifax can cut out Manchester, Oldham and Rochdale if they follow the route given herewith. (A way of reaching York without entering Leeds is given on page 73.)

The starting-point is **Ripponden**, above Sowerby Bridge, south-west of Halifax. From this point the climb of **Blackstone Edge** commences, and beyond Littleborough, on the far (or western) side, there are about two miles of old built-up highway, until the Rochdale by-pass is reached on the left, less than half a mile past the village of Smallbridge.

The by-pass emerges at Castleton, whence the small town of Middleton (where there is an old church and an ancient inn) is gained. In Middleton the way is rightwards to Rhodes and the main entrance to Manchester's great northern 'lung,' **Heaton Park**. At the far end of the wall Sheep Foot Lane turns rightwards, still alongside the park and leads through suburbs, crossing Bury Old Road and Bury New Road, and then dropping down Rainsough Bank to the River Irwell. A steep climb follows, and at the top the way is leftwards to Irlam's o' th' Height, a suburb of Salford. By going rightwards here, the new Liverpool road can be entered where it commences on the left in about 400 yds. This road runs across country to the outskirts of Liverpool, and from its western end there is a fairly simple connection for the Mersey Tunnel, the Wirral Peninsula and North Wales.

An alternative route from Irlam's o' th' Height is to continue across the broad crossroads and follow a minor road to Eccles Old Road, where the way is right into Eccles (famous for both its cakes and its church). In Eccles a left turn goes to **Barton Bridge**, across the Manchester Ship Canal. (Note on the left the famous Bridgewater Canal crossing the Ship Canal.) From this point the route goes by Crofts Bank (where left) to the western outskirts of Stretford and the main Manchester-Chester road through Sale and Altrincham. This provides a further approach to North Wales and (at Mere Corner) a link with the great trunk route that leads southwards to Knutsford, Newcastle-under-Lyme and London, with the branch by Stafford, Wolverhampton, Kidderminster and Worcester for the south-west.

RIVINGTON PIKE AND THE DARWEN MOORS

A few miles north-west of Bolton, on the alternative but more hilly route between that town (the largest *town* in Lancashire) and Preston, is the village of Belmont. Approaching from Bolton, a by-road leads leftwards at the foot of the steep main street and climbs past the church up a stern clough, leaving a dam to the left, to a 'col' (1,062 ft.).

The view westwards from this point on a clear day is widespread, extending right across the low-lying land between Liverpool and Preston to the sea at Southport. By diverging leftwards at the summit the crest of the westerly flank of the range can be reached at the tower of **Rivington Pike**. The stone tower was built in the 18th century. Close to the reservoir at the foot of the hill is a sham castle, modelled on the fortress at Liverpool which was badly damaged in Tudor days. There is a public park of 400 acres, given by the first Lord Leverhulme.

Straight ahead from the fork at the summit mentioned previously the road dips down to the Rivington Reservoirs, in a district full of pretty sights, including woodlands and waterfalls. This stretch of country is quite close to A6, the London-Carlisle road, and can be visited readily from this by turning aside at Adlington Station.

Farther along the Bolton-Belmont-Preston highway, past Belmont Reservoir and at the road summit, a lane strikes rightwards and cuts through some charming half-wild country into the hillside hamlet of **Tockholes**. By turning at the inn and crossroads about 1½ miles ahead, a right turn drops to the Bolton-Darwen-Blackburn road, a less attractive route. Continuing through Pleasington to Mellor Brook by a hilly but varied country road, a link can be made with the Preston-Whalley highway and the Ribble Valley.

Continue to use the Bolton-Belmont-Preston highway as a backbone for side routes. Less than a mile beyond the summit (mentioned previously), at 916 ft., a farmhouse on the right (which bears all the signs of having been an inn) marks the point whence a track goes leftwards, in a westerly direction, past the side of Great Hill and down to the vicinity of the Anglezarke reservoir system at White Coppice, from which it is a short run to the town of Chorley, on A6. This is a pass-storming route, however.

The Preston road from Belmont continues to fall past Abbey Village (alternative name—Withnell) to Riley Green and Hoghton's church. At Hoghton, however, the great sight is the straight, rising drive to Hoghton Tower on the right, which was built in 1565 by Thomas Hoghton. Here James I knighted a loin of beef and called it 'Sirloin', and thus added a new word to the language. Harrison Ainsworth, the Lancashire novelist, mentioned the hall in his works.

Walton-le-Dale and Preston are now a short way ahead, together with the lures of Lakeland, Blackpool and Morecambe.

To the east of the Belmont area there is another stretch of upland, consisting of great bare, shouldering hills. Amongst the 'tit-bits' of this region is the moorland road from the Haslingden Grane-Guide-Blackburn road, just beyond the summit on the Blackburn side, that leads down to Edgworth and to Hawkshaw Lane End. East of the latter, on a southwards thrust of moorland, stands **Holcombe Tower**, above Holcombe Brook, itself high above the Irwell Valley. This is the countryside of Tom Thompson, the contemporary Lancashire dialect writer and broadcaster, who lives close by. The Tower commemorates Sir Robert Peel, the 19th century politician, and was set up in the 1850s. The tower that formerly stood on the opposite side of the Irwell Valley—Grant's Tower—above the Bury-Edenfield road, collapsed some time ago. The name came from the

Scottish brothers Grant, who founded business enterprises in the Irwell Valley, and were immortalized by Dickens as the Cheeryble Brothers in *Nicholas Nickleby*.

South of Hawkshaw Lane End runs a section of Watling Street, on which stands the hilltop village of **Affetside**. West of the Hawkshaw junction runs the valley of the Bradshaw Brook, now badly defiled, that provides, however, a notable piece of path-following between Turton Bottoms and Bradshaw. The mill dams and the woodlands are quite attractive, despite their industrial setting, and there is good riding by a cinder path close to the river. Round to the north-west of Bolton there is similar scenery at the old mill village of Barrow Bridge.

Outstanding among short mid-Lancashire valley explorations is the traversing of the Course of the **Cheesden Brook** from Cheesden, a mere hamlet on the Rochdale-Edenfield road, over Ashworth Moor, by the hostelry of 'Owd Betts', so called from a former owner ('Old Betty'). The Cheesden Brook runs through a quiet pastoral upland countryside, and is followed by cinder lanes and stony tracks that emerge above Hooley Bridge, north of Heywood, which is some ten miles from Manchester.

Short visits to these mid-Lancashire valleys and moors are worth while for wheelmen more concerned about knowing their own countryside than in piling up miles.

Day and Weekend Tours today

York is a designated Cycle City and there are some fantastic National Cycle Network routes to accompany its status. **National Route 65** heading down to Selby is a 15-mile railway path that features an impressive trailing sculpture of the solar system (with the planets dotted along the route at proportioned intervals relative to their distance from each other).

The **National Route 62** is a route for cyclists, walkers and horse riders that connects the Irish and the North Seas. The route enters Selby from the south and then heads east to Hull and the North Sea. From the south it passes through Doncaster on largely traffic-free routes before intersecting with the central part of the Trans Pennine Trail. This central section encompasses a whole network of mostly traffic-free routes in the area, taking in Leeds, Barnsley, Rotherham, Sheffield and Chesterfield. Highlights include **National Route 67** on the bank of Barnsley Canal, which runs through the lovely wooded **Haw Park**. Here there is a link route to **Anglers Country Park**, a hotspot for walking, picnicking, wildlife and bird watching.

Useful maps and books (available from www.sustransshop.co.uk): *Yorkshire Wolds, York & Hull cycle map; Trans Pennine Trail West cycle map; Trans Pennine Trail Central cycle map; Trans Pennine Trail: Official Accommodation & Visitor Guide.*

APPENDIX

Sustrans Cycle Mapping

• View 25,000 miles of cycle routes, including 13,000 miles of National Cycle Network online using Sustrans interactive mapping. Visit: www.sustrans.org.uk/map

You can also:
• Draw your routes, measure distances and share your favourite journey with others.
• Find local amenities including bike shops / hire centres, shops, schools and local attractions.

See every bus stop and train station in the UK with links to their timetables.

The Complete National Cycle Network App

Access our online mapping from your pocket with the Complete National Cycle Network app. The app includes all of our online features as well as:
• GPS tracking – record your route and share it with friends
• Store the map backgrounds for an area when you have no mobile signal

THE LITTLE EXTRA

At a glance there is little to choose between a cycle component made by Walton & Brown and any other. Why, then, have Walton & Brown gained such a world-wide reputation for cycle fittings. The answer to that question is simple enough — no single item ever left the Walton & Brown factory without first having had just that little extra care in the making — the little extra which makes all the difference in quality and appearance, when a machine is running on the road.

WALTON & BROWN LTD.

PHOENIX WORKS, DOWNING STREET, HANDSWORTH, BIRMINGHAM, 21

152

EVER READY

REGD. TRADE MARK

Cycle Lamps and Batteries

When cycling at night let Ever Ready be your guide. There is no more convenient and trouble-free form of cycle lighting than an Ever Ready Battery in an Ever Ready Lamp.

INDEX